Along Life's Way

Along Life's Way

100 Mini-Reflections

J. Vernon Jensen

June 18, 2001

To Bob McKinnell,
valued colleague
"along life's way."

Vern Jensen

VANTAGE PRESS
New York

FIRST EDITION

Copyright © 2001 by J. Vernon Jensen

Published by Vantage Press, Inc.
516 West 34th Street, New York, New York 10001

Manufactured in the United States of America
ISBN: 0-533-13684-9

Library of Congress Catalog Card No.: 00-92275

0 9 8 7 6 5 4 3 2 1

Contents

Preface

As we busily perform our daily tasks and try to fulfill our obligations to self, friends, family, workplace, and society in general, we are increasingly in need of quiet moments of calming reflection and long-range thoughtfulness. We need the long vista to balance the hectic short view. All of us can profit from stimulating, thought provoking musings which can bring comfort, challenge, insight, commitment, pleasure, and new direction-setting.

Through the years I have written brief essays on a variety of subjects dealing with everyday dimensions of life, and have collected one hundred of them for inclusion in this small volume. These self-contained one-page up-beat mini-memoirs could be consumed as one-a-day morsels, or of course combined in whatever quantity and order the reader desires. These essay-ettes discuss single subjects across vastly different areas of life, revealing relationships perhaps not normally considered. I have drawn from my autobiographical experiences, my family life, my many years of teaching university and college students, my travels, my varied readings of Eastern and Western religious and philosophical literature, from sports, and from a variety of other areas of life. A light, humorous touch pokes its nose under the tent occasionally.

The book is aimed at the general thoughtful citizenry of all ages in all walks of life, and it would make an appropriate and welcome gift for birthdays, anniversaries, holidays, graduations, or other occasions.

I wish to dedicate this volume to my family, friends, and colleagues who have walked with me on this journey through life and have enriched my life beyond measure. I especially wish to thank my wife Irene Khin Khin, my son Don, my daughter Maythee, son-in-law John, daughter-in-law Tanya, and grandchildren Sally Kathleen, Danny, Mikey, Ellie, and Dillon.

Along Life's Way

1 / Attachments

Humans need a sense of attachment—to other humans, to a job, to institutions, to nature, to some sense of a Deity. Those without such firm attachments are "at loose ends," are not as fulfilled, adjusted, or effective as they might be. The beauty of friends and family "sticking together" during times of stress is impressive indeed. The loyalty of employees and supervisors to their company and to each other provides a cohesiveness that is crucial to a successful business venture. Teachers firmly committed to their school and their profession experience not only an inner satisfaction but create a superior learning atmosphere for students and build a more healthy society.

Those who sense a closeness to nature experience a pleasure and identity denied to others. Feeling close to some sense of a Deity is central to most religious persuasions.

But all these attachments ought not to be too tight. Spouses need to give each other some breathing space, some freedom to permit their individuality to flourish. Children need to be given the opportunity to break away to some degree from family bonds, to become "independent." One ought not to be too inwardly clinging only to family and a small circle of friends, but should forever seek to expand one's attachments, however, without letting go of existing ones. Job and professional loyalty does not mean we are mindless slaves to the enterprise and that we condone whatever the organization or profession demands. Our love for nature should not make us reclusive. Some religious attachments push adherents to feel they have such a personal attachment to God that they commit horrible acts against those who are outside of their group.

Attachments can indeed be painfully destructive or gloriously constructive. We need to be intelligent and compassionate in our attachments.

1

2 / Balance

Journeying through life we would be wise to balance a number of phenomena. Work and play each have their place, sadness and joy both are to be expected, seriousness and humor are cousins. There is a time to analyze carefully and a time to act boldly. There is a time to reflect on the past and a time to look to the future. Speed and caution both have their time and place. There is "a time to break down and a time to build up" and "a time to keep silence, and a time to speak" (Ecclesiastes 3:3, 7). Strong individualism and commitment to a group are not mutually exclusive.

We need to balance our immersion in the notion that one can't "go home again" with the notion that one "must go home again." That is, for example, college students must realize that they can never fully go back intellectually to their former homes, for maturity and expanding horizons have stretched their visions. Their provincialism has been eroded. But on the other hand, they need to return constantly, in mind if not in body, to their roots, to realize the debt they owe to their heritage, to their parents, to their communities, and to their early schooling. One needs to achieve that balance, which leads one to continue to feel the firmness of the bond, but on a different level.

The admonishment to "go to the ant, thou sluggard" (Proverbs 6:6) needs to be balanced with the plea to see the lilies of the field, which neither toil nor spin. Excessive dwelling on the former can result in neurotic busy-ness, while the latter can be a poetic cover-up for indolence.

Indeed, it is not surprising that our lexicon speaks of dysfunctional people as "unbalanced."

3 / Better and Better?

Growing up on the edge of a small town, my older brother and I during our junior and senior high school years made a vacant lot next to our house into a veritable sports mecca—on a very small and spartan level! For basketball we nailed a big round cheesebox to the wall of a nearby available building. We had a small area where we could play softball. We strung up a net (chicken wire) for tennis, we dug a pit (dirt only) for broadjumping, high jumping, and pole vaulting. Our pole was a limb cut from a tree, rather more crooked and more heavy than bamboo or aluminum poles! We flooded an area in winter by pumping water from our well and carrying bucketsful to create enough ice so we could play broomball. In an adjoining alley, we constructed a sixty-yard dash section, complete with some hurdles.

Each year we added items, so each year I had the feeling that things were inevitably getting better and better, and kids from other parts of town would come to participate on our carefully mowed area with its kept-up facilities.

But my brother and I left after graduation, and upon my return from three years in the army, the area had returned to a jungle state. It struck me forcefully that things don't automatically get better and better; it takes someone's hands, with some skill and much determination. It was a personal awakening to what our generation was experiencing on a national and international level. The nineteenth-century idealism that life on this planet was almost predestined to get better and better was fed by the dramatic advances in science, industry, transportation, democracy, and education, and with flourished moral values seemingly firmly rooted. But the twentieth century was a rude awakening—two world wars and many other major conflicts, totalitarian dictatorships, human rights violations to an incredible degree, depressions, tribal and religious slaughters—demonic acts difficult to comprehend. Better and better?

3

4 / To be Born

What an awesome transition for each of us when we were born! After approximately nine months of developing bone and muscle organs and being, one leaves an interior habitat—warm, dark, quiet, with a life-support system. One enters a new womb—cold, light, noisy—desperately sucking for sustenance. To say we "adjust" to our new surroundings puts it too blandly. We cry, we scream, we grimace, we flail about, we eat, we eliminate. What have we gotten into?

In our new outer space atmosphere, we helplessly exist, confronting huge people, huge things, huge forms. Some inner trust calms us, when in the arms of a few of these huge people. Gentle swaying movement puts us at ease. We get hurt, we heal, we leave scars. We exhaust, we amuse, we enrich our care givers. What limited means yet what fundamental skills for interaction we possess and develop!

Are we as curious about others as they are about us? Our five fingers and five toes, so quickly counted by anxious parents, give immediate evidence of some "normality," gradually confirmed (or discomfirmed) by medical tests. Can we feel the joy of our parents' quiet humming, the tension of their anxiety, the humor of their chuckles? What a strangeness, what an awesomeness in being born!

To those of us who have had the joy of having children and grandchildren, we feel at some inner level of being this awesomeness, and others with strong empathic qualities can also share in this. I write this as our fifth grandchild is entering into our family circle and our world, and the deep thrill is there again, with all its mystery, its excitement, its pleasure, its concerns.

May life be good to you, dearest one, and may you be good to life!

5 / Buffers

Buffers play important roles in many areas of life. Secretaries are buffers between their employers and the public. Lower officials stand between their superiors and the public. Older siblings are buffers between younger siblings and parents. Parents are buffers between their children and old age. Grandparents are buffers between other family members and death, and once they are gone, the psychological shield is removed, leaving younger ones to realize that "we're next."

Priests and others claim to be buffers between believers and God or other spirits. Comedians are buffers between us and sadness; friends are buffers between us and loneliness. Sports are buffers between us and inactivity. Cooks are buffers between us and hunger, and soup kitchens are buffers between the destitute and starvation.

Receptions are buffers between a very happy or sad event and a return to usual routines; for example, following a happy school commencement exercise, following a lovely wedding, or following a sad funeral service.

Real estate agents are buffers between sellers and buyers, and labor negotiators are buffers between contesting parties, as are marriage counselors.

A buffer zone, like the demilitarized zone across the Korean Peninsula for these many years, keeps bitter enemies away from each other. Roofs are buffers between us and the rain, snow or sun.

What don't we owe to buffers! Or do we come to rely too heavily on them?

6 / Caucusing

Life calls for caucusing. The term, Native American in origin, means for a group to come together for counseling among themselves. Political parties have caucuses, and grass-roots democracy depends on groups of committed citizenry with common interests coming together for community improvements. Women form a League of Women Voters, Ladies Aids, Women Historians groups, etc. Men form men's clubs of various types. Boy Scouts and Girl Scouts generate active programs for their members.

Young people need to formulate strategies to employ when dealing with parents or other elders; parents or other adults formulate strategies to employ with children or other youths. Students at all levels seek through their groupings to improve their welfare. Academic or corporate departments strategize on how to secure a larger share of the organization's budget. Football teams "huddle" in a tight circle of secrecy to lay plans for attacking their opponents.

Based on age, gender, social interests, political or social leanings, such caucus groups play a highly necessary and significant role in our lives. The purpose is to vent ideas, sharpen wits, bolster confidence, strengthen and support each other in a private "safe" environment against perceived "foes." Caucuses often seek to correct some perceived unjust treatment, and to plan, crystallize, and execute lines of action. A caucus can ease anxieties, generate enthusiasm, enhance self-esteem, and create bonding.

But some dangers are also present. Members can become trapped in provincial narrow horizons of the caucus, look on outsiders as "enemies," employ incendiary "flaming" language, and become needlessly adversarial. They come to exaggerate their supposed virtues and count loyalty to the in-group to be the highest good.

Drink deeply from the wells of caucuses, but don't become intoxicated.

6

7 / CCC's

In the winter of 1940–41 I spent six months in a Civilian Conservation Corps camp (CCC's) in northern Minnesota. Upon graduating in June 1940 from a small Minnesota high school, I joined the nation's unemployed, and FDR's CCC program during those Depression years came to the rescue of my family and many other families. From one's $30 monthly salary, $22 was sent home to one's dependents.

I learned a number of helpful lessons in the C's:

1. "You can't see the forest for the trees" took on a fresh and deeper meaning. Our major task, pruning pine trees in the Superior National Forest on snow shoes with nearly frozen feet and snow and sawdust coming down one's neck, brought me too close to the trees to really appreciate their extent and beauty. One Sunday I climbed a forest ranger tower in the vicinity and got a long-distance view of the forest and terrain. I could see more clearly what those individual trees were a part of, and it made my subsequent labors more meaningful.

2. I learned to understand and appreciate people from varying backgrounds, for about one-third of us were from Minnesota small towns, about one-third from the inner cities of St. Paul and Minneapolis, and about one-third from the rural hills of Arkansas.

3. Discovering that a very small number had graduated from high school, I realized how fortunate I had been to get a solid educational foundation.

4. I learned to adapt to the rigors of hard labor in sub-zero conditions, and to the expectations and responsibilities of communal life.

5. It reinforced our high school senior class's motto, the familiar adage, "If we rest, we rust," for our forestry supervisor constantly reminded us never to sit and rest if we got tired in the woods, for we would likely fall asleep and freeze to death. If you rest, you die.

7

8 / Not too Close, Not too Far

In the Hebrew Book of Ecclesiastes, we are admonished not to stand too near the rich man, lest he destroy us, but not too far, lest he forget us. The Hindu god Krishna is portrayed in the *Bhagavad Gita* as pervading all of life and yet unattached from all of life. Parents, teachers, employers, and counselors need to get close to, but not too close to their children, students, employees, and counselees.

Husbands and wives would do well to remember the words of the twentieth-century Lebanese poet and mystic Kahlil Gibran: "Let there be spaces in your togetherness . . . even as the strings of a lute are alone though they quiver with the same music. . . . And stand together, yet not too near together, for the pillars of the temple stand apart, and the oak tree and the cypress grow not in each other's shadow."

The twentieth-century literary giant in India, Rabindranath Tagore (1961) wrote: "In every kind of love there should be a certain amount of separation and detachment. No good ever comes of completely swamping each other." In a television interview, newscaster and novelist, Jim Lehrer, said in a loving manner of himself and his wife, also a writer: "We live our separate lives together." Jawaharlal Nehru and his daughter Indira, separated by his imprisonment in India by the British (both became prime ministers of India), reveal a meaningful closeness highlighted by the title of the book, *Two Alone, Two Together*.

Boyfriends and girlfriends need to experience closeness, but not to the point of violating each other's sanctity. Athletes know that in defending against an opponent on the basketball court, you need to be close enough to reduce his/her effectiveness, but not so close that she/he can outmaneuver you. We enjoy sitting close to a fireplace or a campfire, but not so close as to be uncomfortable.

Indeed, in much of life, it is important to be close but not too close, far but not too far.

9 / Clouds

We live out our days on this earth under a canopy of clouds. Their presence serves as a central metaphor, depicting various moods and qualities and situations. William Wordsworth's "I wandered lonely as a cloud" is reminiscent of one of the ancient Hindu scriptures, the *Bhagavad Gita*, when it comments on disconnectedness, stating that one feels "like a broken cloud, having severed its allegiance, and yet having failed to gain a new one, come(s) to nothing and melt(s) away to nothingness" (Ramacharaka, 1935, p. 78).

This feeling of aloneness, of being separated from others, is a powerfully depressing sensation. We speak of dark clouds hanging over us, keeping us depressed, or on the horizon as war or other highly dangerous events seem to be approaching. Of course, the modern metaphor of a mushroom cloud speaks of Armageddon. Yet dark clouds, with their life-giving moisture, also speak of hope to farmers gazing at their parched fields. The "silver lining" also speaks of hope.

When something is unclear, whether because of a physical condition (e.g., a cataract) or whether intellectually, we say our vision or our understanding is cloudy. When we suddenly achieve an understanding of something, we "pierce the clouds."

Clouds are assumed to be an anomaly, infringing on the normality of a clear sky; thus, weather forecasters usually speak of "partly cloudy" weather, seldom "partly clear" skies. We can read into clouds shapes and formations what we will. For example, one person may be reminded of a concrete, specific thing, whereas someone else may think of some intangible abstraction. People who live in large open spaces, e.g., "The Big Sky" country or near large bodies of water, have a deeper appreciation for clouds and their actual or metaphorical impact on us. Far above us, the unreachable touches our interaction with life in many dimensions.

10

10 / Concentration

"I can't concentrate" is a familiar lament of many. We admire those who seem to have the ability to channel all their attention and energies to some task at hand, whether it is playing chess, cooking, building something, repairing an object, fishing, reading or writing.

What a remarkable evolution we have seen with the advent of the computer culture, where now thousands (millions?) of rigid people sit motionless, Buddhalike, staring into a computer screen, concentrating 100 percent on its changing images. Many (most?) of those people probably at one time claimed they couldn't concentrate on anything! The combined visual and print mediums of the computer, its ease and speed, its simplicity in correcting errors, and the excitement of creating something and/or conversing with others in distant places simply leads people to realize that indeed they *can* concentrate.

Television and radio, however, with their sound bites and rapid shifting from one unrelated topic to another, fill our minds with incoherent mosaics, reducing our concentration skills.

To give one's complete attention to some person is a precious encounter in life; hence small grandchildren and grandparents love each other so dearly, for each has the time and desire to give full attention to the other.

On a sharply different level, our century has witnessed the unbelievably barbaric "concentration camps," where vulnerable people were sent and where most met their death. People are concentrated on subways, in sports stadiums, in mass meetings of many types. Concentration of a single person's mind or of a coming together of thousands of bodies play important roles as we go through life.

11 / Confession

The beginning of moral and intellectual growth is confession. Many religious worship services always begin with a group confessional statement, an acknowledgment of "sin," of moral shortcomings, with the understanding that higher moral behavior moves on from that point, that a better life can hardly result until that first base has been touched. Some religious frameworks include a personal confessional procedure, an enclosed box in which a confession is made in secret and confidence to a professional confessor. These institutional confessional arrangements can be very helpful, but the ultimate is that people confess inwardly to themselves, with no ritual needed.

When students make a decision to enter a college or university, they are really also making a confession, an acknowledgment that they have intellectual shortcomings—be it in biology, logic, history, literature, etc. They even pay a hefty tuition to have their ignorance reduced! Students who think they "know it all" from the start, who have not touched the first base of admitting their intellectual shortcomings, are sadly misleading themselves, and their low ceilings will be far short of what their potential could be.

The call for quotas to balance a former injustice is really a society's confession of guilt, an admission that it hasn't been fair to some of its members in the past. By establishing and maintaining a quota arrangement, society brings into being a more just balance, though some critics say it creates a new imbalance. Without the quota, its defenders assert, the likelihood of correction for past injustices becomes much less certain.

Confessing moral failings clears one's soul, one's being, enabling new beginnings. Confessing intellectual failings clears one's mind, generating an impetus for deeper scholarly inquiry.

12 / Cosmopolitanism

To possess a mind-set that leaves one feeling at home with all other humans on this planet, at one with the cosmos, defines the spirit of cosmopolitanism. It says that narrow-minded provincialism is too confining, too corroding of the human spirit, too costly. The former U.S.S.R. used to label their dissident citizens as "homeless cosmopolitans," those who were not sufficiently loyal to their "home" country, not fully obedient to Communist dictates. Communist myopia couldn't bear to look beyond their own doctrinaire precinct of existence.

As a graduate student, I was active in the "Cosmopolitan Club," approximately half of which consisted of foreign students and half from America. It enabled me to establish friendships with others from many parts of the world, some of whom became life-long friends and correspondents, who helped me have a broader and richer outlook on life.

It has been said that the Indus River is the most cosmopolitan water system in the world, with streams beginning in Tibet, flowing for nineteen hundred miles through Pakistan and India, and emptying into the Arabian Sea. It gives more water to a greater number of races and religions and peoples than any other river system, and in its journey, it cares not about the local provincialisms.

Fukuzawa Yukichi, the renowned cosmopolitan leader of Westernization in late nineteenth-century Japan, expressed in his autobiography late in life his evolving outlook: "My life [which began] in the restricted conventions of the small Nakatsu clan was like being packed tightly in a lunch box. . . . Reading strange books, associating with new kinds of people, working with all the freedom never dreamed of before, traveling abroad two or three times, finally [I] came to find even the empire of Japan too narrow for [my] domain. What a merry life this has been!" May we all sense this joy as we live out our existence as adventurous and responsible people on this small globe spinning through the cosmos.

13 / Cover-up

In cold climes, to cover up one's body and face from low temperatures and bitter winds is a necessity. In many areas of life, we employ the "cover-up" as a solution to a social or political problem. We close the closet door so visitors can't see the mess inside, we hang a picture over a damaged area on the wall, we build a fence to hide our view of a neighbor's junky yard (or their view of our junky yard). Deodorants minister to our desire to cover up unpleasant body odors, and the cosmetic industry glories in our desire to cover up unattractive facial features. A familiar idiom is that to get rid of a problem, we "sweep it under the rug"—out of sight, out of mind.

Sometimes the cover-up is meant to be a temporary solution, but at other times it is meant to be the final solution. Skilled carpenters learn how to cover up uneven cuts with molding trim or other techniques.

In public affairs, we frequently accuse officials or law-enforcement officers of a cover-up, of keeping from the public eye some questionable action, thus giving it a definite negative connotation, bordering on the illegal. Investigative journalism thrives on ferreting out such hidden situations.

We criticize others for covering up, but we often rush to do it ourselves. We at times appropriately cover up our deep disappointments, our aches and pains, our worries. We may, for instance, use the radio or recordings to mask our loneliness or other discomforts. At other times, cover-ups would be unwise escapism, unhealthy for ourselves and others. Flattery at times is a cover-up for one's true feelings about someone.

To know when to cover up and when not to is one of those important insights to learn on life's journey.

14 / Creators

We bask in the performance of beautiful music and all but ignore the person who created it. We dig into delicious bakery goodies, but we seldom think about the baker. Elegant woodworking we admire, but we think very little about the craftsman. Architects and construction firms are often overlooked or soon forgotten, unless their structure is of special importance. Clothes designers go unheralded as we parade their garments. We drink in a lovely landscaped area and flower gardens, but we don't ponder over the person(s) who brought them into being.

We may occasionally think about all of creation, but we do not have a deep sense of awe as to the creator behind it all, even if it is only the abstract "big-bang" theory. An ancient Chinese proverb is a good guide: "One thinks of the source of the stream as one takes a drink from it."

Since the creators are often invisible, we do not take them into our consciousness as much as we should in our limited, myopic view of things around us. We need to honor the sources more deeply, even if it is only an imaginative venture.

15 / Criticism

We constantly evaluate life around us. We judge the actions, statements, ideas, and clothing of those with whom we come in contact. We pronounce a scene beautiful, a building ugly. We judge newspapers, magazines, books, and television programs. We assess musical renditions, art productions, and motion pictures. We judge the local baseball team and the quality of food in a particular restaurant. We evaluate the speech of some politician or the comments of an acquaintance.

"Criticism" thus is synonymous with "judging," "evaluating," "assessing,"—perceiving strengths and weaknesses. It is seeing both the good and bad aspects, not just the negative items, which is how the word is usually employed in our colloquial usage.

Wise parents seek to fulfill their role by providing both negative admonitions and helpful praise to their children. College and university students on their own initiative place themselves in a position in which they will be criticized, evaluated, judged. Aspiring figure skaters, tennis players, or golfers seek out professional coaches, who can give rigorous evaluation leading to significant improvement.

Being willing to accept criticism, indeed to seek it out, is a sign of maturity, a crucial step to bettering ourselves. When we have found a wise and compassionate criticizer, we have indeed found a jewel of great value.

But we need to evaluate with care the evaluators. The writer of Ecclesiastes gave wise guidance: "It is better to hear the rebuke of the wise, than for a man to hear the song of fools" (7:5).

We need to become wise criticizers of ourselves, to be willing to see and correct our failings, to maintain our strengths, and to move on to higher heights.

16 / Debate

Democracies have a core value of honoring discussion and debate as a procedure of operating in the public decision-making sphere. The assumption is that wiser decisions are made for the benefit of society, and individual dignity is enhanced. Many voices freely expressed and vigorously interacting will be better than relying on the supposed superior wisdom of one powerful person or group, of some all-knowing hierarchical party or leader. The ancient democratic Athenians, Pericles asserted, "instead of looking on discussion as the stumbling-block in the way of action . . . think it an indispensable preliminary to any wise action at all" (Thucydides).

Many times, of course, we despair of the time-consuming wrangling in democratic legislative bodies, and think of them as directionless and noisy cacophonies, but we ought to remember Winston Churchill's remark that "parliamentary government is the worst of all possible forms of government, until we look at the alternatives."

Most of our school systems take pride in teaching students to debate, either in classes or in extracurricular contexts. Whether debate is the form of structure advocacy on a specific proposition, or in a more informal wide-ranging clash of ideas, its values are indeed great. It stresses rigorous research, careful preparation, sound reasoning, sufficient evidence of high quality to support claims, the ability to refute the opposition, and effective speaking. Potential dangers were expressed tellingly by Richard Whately, an early nineteenth-century British rhetorical theorist: "When young men's faculties are in an immature state, and their knowledge scanty, crude, and imperfectly arranged, if they are prematurely hurried into a habit of fluent elocution, they are likely to retain through life a careless facility of pouring forth ill-digested thoughts in well-turned phrases, and an aversion to cautious reflection." Indeed, thoughtful solid substance should take precedence.

17 / Debtors

The minute we come into this world, we are debtors. We owe our very being to our parents and the life-giving force behind all existence. We owe much to the medical monitoring during pregnancy and delivery. We receive nurturing from parents, family, and society. Schools are there, waiting for us to enter. Up through high school, we have received virtually everything free. With the exception of some income from part-time jobs, we haven't paid for the food on the table, for our medical needs, for our clothing, for our participation in sports or various other activities. Soon we begin to earn part or all of our living costs, and eventually, if we are at all sensitive, we begin thinking of paying back to society, even if only in some small, often indirect, way.

In my case, I received much. My mother got a small widow's pension from the state, we got county welfare assistance in order to have a housekeeper during mother's many bedridden years, and I received the advantages of free public education. Upon discharge from the army following World War II, the GI Bill enabled me to go into graduate studies. Often I have reflected on what life would have been like without those societal aids, those "loans."

Without being presumptuous, I have tried to pay back society by attempting to be a responsible citizen, and I have looked on my profession of college and university teaching as a meaningful avenue of service. It has enabled me to participate in the nurturing of the fine youth in our society, and hopefully to contribute in some small way to enriching their lives and their contributions in turn to society.

Surely no person is an island. As debtors we ought to gladly pay back at least a portion of our "loan" in whatever ways seem available to us as we go through life, not in any sense of a morbid obligation, but in a joyful response to the gifts that we have received from others, many unseen, many unknown.

19

18 / Decision-Making

One of the marks of a mature person is to be a wise decision-maker. At the core of parenting is to inculcate wise decision-making standards in their offspring. Parents earnestly hope that their children will make wise choices in selecting their friends, their activities, their jobs, their educational goals, their spouses, their basic values. How much anguish does a parent experience when they see that their children don't measure up! How much suffering do we all experience when we realize we have made an unwise choice, taken a wrong fork in the road along life's way, selected a needlessly bumpy trail!

In interactions with others, we all have our own styles of decision-making. Some individuals and groups seem to have the ability to make wise decisions rapidly, with assurance, harmony, and with good results. Others need more time to deliberate, to scrutinize all factors laboriously, and have difficulty in controlling tensions and ill-will. Whatever the style, we need to honor the importance of wise decision-making in life, and to train and discipline ourselves to be good exemplars.

We need to warn ourselves constantly of undue haste or delay in decision-making. Once decisions are made, we need the fortitude to live up to their demands and live with their effects.

Those people in society identified as decision-makers often wield considerable power. For example, members of legislatures on the state or national level are courted by hordes of lobbyists who seek decisions favoring their interests. Academic deans and department chairs, who often make crucial decisions on personnel and budget matters, accumulate considerable power, and ex-deans and ex-department chairs discover with chagrin how rapidly that power evaporates!

19 / Desires

Humans have many desires, beginning with satisfying elementary physical comforts and pleasures. We desire emotional and psychological comforts, which might be summarized in an ascending hierarchy: (1) the desire to be *noticed* (hence, we call attention to ourselves, go to social functions, etc.); (2) the desire to be *wanted* (we seek employment, membership in clubs, athletic teams, etc.); (3) the desire to be *liked* (hence a speaker includes humor, a child obeys a parent, an employee cooperates with peers and supervisors, etc.); (4) the desire to be *loved* (that mutual nurturing relationship between intimates, hence courtship and marriage).

Unfortunately, these powerful desires often can be so overwhelming that individuals and society are severely damaged. We can become their virtual slaves.

Most religions, especially Hinduism and Buddhism, but also Judaism, Christianity, and Islam, make much of renunciation of desires. While that emphasis can be helpful in creating a more humane and harmonious existence for all concerned, it sometimes can get carried to unhealthy extremes, especially with powerful organizational authority behind it.

Legalistic and ritualistic suppression of desires, motivated by fear or blind obedience to some doctrinaire demands, hardly is healthy behavior. It is probably more healthy to think in terms of managing, of channeling, of controlling these fundamental yearnings of human nature, so that these desires can contribute to the well-being of individuals and society.

20 / Dialogue

In many different contexts, we speak of the importance of dialogue. A healthy family, we say, is one in which parents and children are engaging in free and open dialogue with each other. A productive workplace is one in which workers and management exchange ideas in an ongoing dialogue. Professions wishing to maintain and improve their edge of excellence need free-flowing dialogue within their membership and with those whom they serve.

A democratic society depends on its elected officials and citizens being willing to engage in dialogue in the formulation and enforcement of rules and regulations for living together. A healthy and cohesive society needs frank and empathic dialogue among its groups and factions.

The dialogical spirit is one, then, which reflects openness, frankness, empathy, freedom, ongoingness, genuineness, respect, responsibility, mutual support and trust. It listens respectfully to the other participants. It seeks to enter into the other person's position.

For example, a helpful guide for Christians and Muslims to engage in fruitful dialogue would be for each to state at the outset three things that they like about the other religion and three things they dislike about their own. Usually we reverse that, for we are quick to see our own perceived virtues and the perceived faults of the other. Such a simple procedure may be the beginning of a surprising oneness between two parties that initially felt divided by a huge chasm.

Readers will be able to supply numerous examples from their own situations in which the dialogical spirit could make life more harmonious, meaningful, productive, pleasant, and enriching.

21 / Discrimination

In going through life, we have to discriminate. When buying foods we discriminate in their quality and price. Parents admonish their children to choose their friends carefully. In selecting our spouses, we need to discriminate with great care based on common values and interests.

In choosing a college, we discriminate in terms of its prestige, locality, faculty, cost, and facilities. Graduate school admissions committees select and reject applicants on the basis of their past grades, special admissions test results, and other criteria.

Society puts in place age discrimination guides, so that youngsters have to wait until a certain age of maturity before they can get a driver's license, purchase tobacco or alcohol, or can vote.

I am not allowed to play on my grandson's Little League baseball teams—age discrimination! Chinese restaurants understandably choose waitpersons of a Chinese heritage as part of the establishment's motif.

But our discriminating should be meaningful and just. The horrible slavery legacy of the United States has lingered, making complete equality in employment, housing, educational opportunities, and other facets of life still far from equal between blacks and whites. Some whites now claim reverse discrimination is hurting their opportunities in employment (but hardly in choice of housing). The Anglo majority has not reached out in full equality to those of Asian, Hispanic, Native American, and other minority heritages, despite some conscientious efforts in the last half of the twentieth century. Sexual orientation and disabilities are also factors that have brought much unfair discrimination.

Surely a mature and compassionate society needs to operate its discriminatory practices in a meaningful, fair, just, open, and humane fashion.

23

22 / Distance Breeds Mystique

The further away from the ruled, the ruler acquires more mystique. The ruler is given, or usurps, moral and leadership qualities bordering on the mystical. The mayor of a small town isn't expected to be a glorious leader or moral guide—just take care of the roads, sewer, water, fire and police, public park, and festivals. The parents, clergy, teachers, and general citizenry will take care of moral and intellectual guidance, thank you very much.

But when we relate to distant national rulers, a quantum leap is taken, even in a democracy. We expect, unrealistically and unfairly and dangerously, that the president and other high officials are all-knowing, all-wise, and represent high virtue. We slip into ancient and medieval mind-sets, which link judge and priest, theocratic molds of various types, secular power with religious power, leading to a metaphorical mystique, usually for more ill than good.

The palatial isolation of ancient Egyptian Pharaohs, Roman, Chinese and Japanese emperors, European monarchs, modern Fascist and Communist emperors, Popes in Rome and Avignon, illustrate this granting and/or usurpation of veneration to the person at the distant top of the pyramid. A little Toto (*Wizard of Oz*) often is needed to pull aside the curtain, revealing the sham of the mystique.

We likewise seem to want or expect those at the top of the entertainment or sports world to be moral role models. The great tennis player Arthur Ashe (1993) warned young people: "We . . . think of . . . basketball players and pop singers as possible role models, when nothing could be further, in most cases, from their capabilities."

Indeed, let the village mayor take care of the roads, and leave the moral role modeling to those who qualify for the assignment.

23 / Dreams

Our dreams during our sleeping hours are often strange mixtures of the enjoyable and the depressing. Their meaning has mystified humans since the dawn of time, and those who claimed to be able to interpret dreams often acquired enormous power with rulers and the general populace. During our waking hours, we "day dream," losing ourselves in a private world.

The American Dream continues to draw immigrants to our shores in their search for freedom, equality, and opportunity. They bring a willingness to work hard for fulfillment of this dream, if not for themselves, then surely for their children.

We dream of what we wish life would be. Our minds are stretched to visualize some ideal situation. Martin Luther King, Jr.'s "I Have a Dream" oration in Washington, D.C., in August of 1963, was a litany of what he felt American society could one day become, when racial discrimination in all its forms and tyrannies would vanish and a just society would take its place. "I have a dream today," he thundered in graceful, rhythmic repetition, and decades later, we are lifted by his words and dreams.

Youths dream of independence from adult controls. Parents dream of the best kind of futures for their children. When dreams come true, we rejoice.

But what of this human capacity to dream? Psychologists are hard at work trying to understand it, and someday perhaps we will come close to comprehending the dream world. But in the meantime, we can continue to dare to dream of the implementation of our ideals.

What kind of dreams do we have for ourselves, for our loved ones, and for society in general? Our answer to that question will define who we are.

24 / Education

Wise societies make education mandatory for their youth, knowing its fundamental importance for individual maturity and societal advancement. A Jewish proverb (Harris, 1901) put forth a challenge: "A town which has no school should be abolished." Educational institutions bring together not merely bodies but minds, where students and teachers engage in development of intellect and spirit.

Individuals need to be eager to learn if real education is to occur. Another Jewish proverb (Harris, 1901) prods us: "Be eager to acquire knowledge; it does not come to thee by inheritance." Confucius (VIII, 17) put it this way: "Learn as if you were following someone (with) whom you could not catch up, as though it were someone you were frightened of losing." Confucius (VII, 8) minced no words in selecting his students: "Only one who bursts with eagerness do I instruct."

What does it mean to be educated? One short summary might be to say one learns to observe, analyze, synthesize, and communicate. That is, one improves one's ability to "see" things, to secure data. One sharpens one's ability to evaluate the data and the assumptions and reasoning that become part of the body of knowledge with which one is dealing. One learns to put it all together in some meaningful, organized, coherent synthesis. Finally, one improves one's ability to communicate more clearly and effectively one's findings, one's knowledge, to others.

One acquires skills and values. Long ago Confucius (XV, 9) asserted: "A craftsman, if he means to do good work, must first sharpen his tools." Undeveloped talents cannot accomplish the task and are a sad waste of human resources. But acquisition of skills needs to be accompanied by commitment to humane values, lest those very skills merely develop sophisticated thieves. Training intellectual giants who are moral pygmies is hardly a worthy enterprise.

25 / Empathy

To interact to the highest degree of oneness with others demands empathy. This calls for careful listening, for understanding, identifying with, and respecting the perspectives, assumptions, feelings, and rights of others. It demonstrates the ability to understand "where they are coming from," "their point of view," or better yet, their "place of view."

Parents lying on the floor with their small child see the room's surroundings from the place of view of the offspring, and as the child grows through the teenage years, sensitive and wise parents continue to try to see things from their children's place of view.

High quality teachers are sensitive to the level of knowledge, interest, and anxiety of their students. Humane employers understand the concerns and needs of their employees.

Trying to enter into the world of others—their views, their desires, their motives, their hopes—to walk for a period of time in the moccasins of the other person, as the Native American adage puts it, is not as easy as it may seem. Indeed, we probably can never enter *completely* into their world, but we can strive for a *reasonable zone of empathy*, which enables us to interact not only more effectively but more humanely with others.

We, as well as the other parties, will reap highly significant benefits. For example, we lose much of our provincialism, we get out of our confining shell, and we see the world with a more holistic perspective. We come out of close-mindedness to a more openness. The other participants feel a considerable measure of contentment, sensing that their place of view has been explored and appreciated.

26 / Emptiness

Different kinds of emptiness impact on us as we go through life. At times we have experienced a sense of emptiness when what we are saying and doing seems to have little meaning to us or to others. When a close friend moves away, we grieve over the void in our life. When children leave home for college or employment, parents experience the emptiness of the house—along with the freedom of the empty nest!

When a public speech lacks significant content, we say it is empty. The Book of Job (35:16) expressed such shallowness well: "Therefore doth Job open his mouth in vanity; he multiplieth words without knowledge." The poet John Greenleaf Whittier (1892) wrote of his desire to flee from vain philosophers who "baffled ever, babble still."

How we approach emptiness can be highly important. For example, the familiar definition of an optimist is one who views a glass not as half empty, but as half full. Indeed, emptiness can be a challenge, a prod to fill a space or period of time with meaningful substance.

Unfortunately, some youth—and some adults—decide to fill their emptiness with self-destructive activities, which also harm society. Thus, how we choose to fill the emptiness in our lives is a crucial decision for all of us throughout our journey.

27 / Exits

Exits are very important. Prior to take-off, the flight attendant urges the passengers to note where the exits are in case of emergency. Arriving at our hotel room, we check the nearest exits in case of fire. On freeways, exit ramps are designated in large, easy-to-read signs.

Numerous verbal and nonverbal acts signal leave-taking in communicative situations. In interpersonal communication, for example, such phrases as "see you soon" or "have a good day," and a smile or a hug may mark the exiting. The parting statements or gestures between parents and children when the latter leave for college, distant employment, or foreign travel, usually become deeply embedded in their memories. When anger or hatred dominate the exiting, resulting in demeaning language or gestures, such a suture may be very difficult to heal.

Deathbed communicative acts—as the "final exit" draws near—are full of the most intense feelings possible, as we walk down that final corridor of life with a loved one. Simply touching that person fulfills a bonding and says all that can or needs to be said.

Business corporations all too often downsize the number of employees with brusk termination notices, with little or no compassion, usually justified with the sanctimonious claim that they are merely obeying the Market God who honors leanness, efficiency, and profits. A cartoon in the *New Yorker* captured the essence: a supervisor comes into an employee's office and says, "As of noon today, you're fired. In the meantime, keep up the good work." Quite different exit messages are given by the more humane organizations which arrange for exit interviews with, and provide counseling services for, departing employees.

Like actors on a stage, we need to make appropriate and graceful exits.

29

28 / The Fun of Flinging

Some time ago I noticed a couple of neighborhood children gaily flinging stones over a nearby garage, apparently with little concern for where, on what or whom, these missiles would fall. They seemed swept up in the fun of the moment, with little thought for the potentially serious consequences. I blushingly remembered somewhat similar youthful activities in my own past.

People in some turbulent areas of the globe enjoy flinging stones at law-enforcement personnel or vehicles, but they loudly denounce any retaliation (which admittedly usually is excessive and decidedly more deadly). Some folks love to fling at, but don't like to be "flung" at.

Once a basketball fan, in the heat of reacting to an official's call, threw an object onto the court, narrowly missing some players. One player picked it up and threw it back at the spectator, who then angrily charged toward the court, gesturing wildly in a threatening manner.

A small child enjoys flinging toys and all available small objects out of the crib and around the room. Many children and adults often fling epithets at others, with little concern for the hurt that they are bringing to the recipients. Employers fling rude comments at employees, and insensitive teachers fling barbed criticisms at their students. Military units engage in flinging deadly missiles, insensitive to the devastation and suffering that results "over there."

We seem to slide over much too easily the fact that acts have consequences, that "flinging" ends up affecting someone at the receiving end. Surely we need to remind ourselves that a healthy society depends on all of us being sensitive to the results of our flinging.

29 / Freedom

Basic freedoms are at the heart of American democracy. The First Amendment to the Constitution protects our freedom of religion, speech, press, peaceful assembly, and petition for redress of grievances. The Fifth Amendment enunciates our freedom not to speak in a self-incriminating context. We feel that freedom of initiative on the part of the citizenry, rather than waiting for government to legislate, is a healthy generating force for progress and societal well-being.

We emphasize giving our children as much freedom as seems wise for them to develop and mature. In academia the fresh air of freedom is at the core of scholarly research and classroom teaching. In the business sector, we emphasize freedom of enterprise, along with, of course, reasonable governmental regulations for the protection and well-being of society.

But freedom should not be thought of as some parochial American value. It is a universal urge, a universal right. Freedom from constraint of some tightly structured societal body is yearned for by the more mature among us. For example, Tagore (1961) expressed his enlightened family's freedom from the shackles of orthodox Hinduism: "We were ostracized because of our heterodox opinions about religion; therefore, we enjoyed the freedom of the outcaste."

Martin Luther King, Jr., concluding his "I Have a Dream" speech, looked to the time when blacks and others suffering from discrimination, could utter, "free at last, free at last, thank God Almighty, free at last!"

It is a goal, it is a process, it is a precious jewel. Use it or lose it. Misuse it, and we will also lose it.

30 / Gardening

To engage in gardening is to bring together both the feeling of freedom and the sense of responsibility. To be in the openness of a garden area, to be free from constraints of other humans, to be free to deposit your choice of seeds, to grow what you will, is an invigorating sense of freedom. It provides the fun and awe of seeing growth take place, slowly and silently, before your very eyes. It relieves worries and tensions as you tend to the bits and pieces of the botanical world. It gives peace of mind. The result can be a precise, structured, planned garden, or a more informal patchwork of various items. Each have their unique beauty.

But gardening ties you down, putting you on an uncompromising schedule, a firm commitment to do as your creatures demand. You do not just sow the seeds and walk away to return in a couple of months. You carefully nurture the small plants, feed their thirst, prune their excessive siblings, eliminate competing weeds, tie up weak stems and branches, and harvest their fruits at the appropriate time. In short, it takes rigorous attention, constant care.

It is well to decide before you begin, whether you are willing to become a responsible caregiver to the enterprise. If not, spend your time and seek your pleasures elsewhere.

Gardening is a familiar and meaningful metaphor in many areas of life. Teachers, for example, are spoken of as gardeners, who seek to enable youth to grow to maturity, to nourish them, to extract weeds from their paths, to see them advance intellectually slowly but perceptively over a period of time. Proselytizing religions view themselves as planting the seeds of their faith, nurturing young recruits, and looking forward to an eventual bountiful harvest. Business leaders rigorously tend to their resources with an eye on reaping an abundant profit.

31 / Gifts

A gift is that which is given voluntarily. We give gifts at designated times—at birthdays, school graduations, religious holidays, wedding anniversaries, retirement parties. We give gifts to social projects, educational enterprises, medical research, religious organizations, public radio and television, and political parties. At its purest, the motivation is simply the desire to make someone happy or to enrich society, without any personal gain except an inner satisfaction of having contributed.

While gift-giving theoretically does not call for something in return, it often does expect some reciprocation, if not immediately, then in the long run. In the political arena, corporations or wealthy individuals give gifts to political leaders in expectation of some favorable legislation. The distinction between gifts and bribes often becomes difficult to ascertain, especially so in some cultures. But while gift-giving can take on negative connotations and be tarnished by certain usages, it nevertheless remains one of the central blessings of life, to giver and receiver alike.

Devoted spouses are grateful for the gift of each other, and proud parents revel in the gift of mature and loving children. The gift of good health is a prized possession. We are mindful of the gift of good friends and fellowship, and of the very gift of life itself.

Gifts are also attributes possessed. We speak of the managerial gifts of a skilled executive, and the gifts of excellent teachers, doctors, public speakers, musicians, artists, and athletes.

These two dimensions come together when a gifted person freely shares those gifts, whatever they may be. The ancient assertion reverberates: it is better to give than to receive.

32 / Gown-in-Town

For over three decades, I have belonged to a faculty dining club at the University of Minnesota, which meets monthly, October through June. It is a broad interdisciplinary group, with members coming from all areas, such as engineering, law, medicine, agriculture, physics, political science, history, literature, communication, ecology, genetics, to name a few. It is a healthy monthly reminder of the many areas of knowledge about which one is quite ignorant, a helpful humbling experience for professors! Members take their turn to report on their research interests, followed by audience participation. Our guests often include visiting professors, some from foreign countries, and spouses.

The name comes from the fact that our club, which began in 1914, meets off campus, in a hotel or for a long time now in the Minneapolis or St. Paul AAUW (American Association of University Women) building. To the founders, it brought to mind medieval Oxford and Cambridge, when the students, identified by their gowns, made their presence felt throughout those towns, and historically the friction between students and townspeople became very troublesome. Fortunately our Gown-in-Town has no such ill-will with the community!

Some of my closest faculty friends have been formed in this club, and it has come to symbolize what a university ought to be, an exchanging of research findings and speculations and interests across the whole landscape of academia. It builds a meaningful sense of belonging to a cohesive entity instead of some sprawling, disconnected, unrelated specialties and departments.

I would hope that such dining clubs are successfully operating in many universities, and I would hope that corporations or other institutions throughout society would also have similar, regularized, mutually satisfying exchange of ideas among its members.

33 / HQ

IQ (Intelligence Quotient) tests are familiar to us all. In addition, students desiring to attend colleges and universities take special exams to test their intellectual capabilities to help predict their likelihood of succeeding. Applicants for graduate school take a GRE (Graduate Record Exam), which is one guide among others, such as past grades and recommendations, for the admissions committee to decide who shall be permitted to enroll. An important dimension is not included in these measuring and predicting procedures.

I would rather facetiously suggest an HQ (Hunger Quotient) test. Surely a central factor is the degree of eagerness of the applicants for the rigors and commitment of higher education. How hungry are they? It would be good if we could measure it! If that eagerness isn't high enough, they may we be wasting their time and money, as well as the resources of the institution and of the parents or others who are helping them.

One of the glories of having older students come back to the college classroom is that they usually are extremely eager, highly motivated, desperately hungry for that educational opportunity that they missed earlier in life.

In the absence of an HQ test, all applicants would be wise to look into themselves and estimate their own hunger level. This process applies not only to those applying for entry into higher education, but to all walks of life as well. Before we set out on any journey, we ought to ask ourselves just how eager we are, how hungry we are, to undertake this venture. This assumes that we are fully convinced that the destination, the goal, is one worthy of our hunger pangs.

34 / Imagining

The capacity of human beings to imagine, to enter into some other existence through mental maneuverings, is said to be one of the factors distinguishing us from other animals.

The power of fictional literature stimulates us to enter into the lives of other people. We gladly acquiesce in its enticement to imagine ourselves as someone else, in a different place and time. The enormous appeal of fictional space travel, of *Star Trek* and other such adventures, is testimony to the human capacity and desire to imagine beyond our known mileau, to engage in the free flow of thought and yet to harness that thought into a coherent parameter. We joyfully dream of life "somewhere over the rainbow." It has even led to group suicides, sending members on their imaginary flight into space.

Role-playing by children or adults is an illustration of the human capacity to imagine themselves as someone else. Watching small children carry on imaginary conversations with someone on toy telephones or with stuffed animals is an intriguing phenomenon. In playful moods children of all ages pretend to be dogs or other animals.

Religions have created imaginary heavens and hells, transmigrations into animals, and all sorts of existences after death, and, drawing on fear, have deeply ingrained these visualizations into the minds of those who believe their pronouncements. Make-believe worlds become institutionalized.

In recent years women deeply interested in religion, especially within the Christian framework, have organized a "re-imagining" effort, to reconceptualize many of the male-oriented images of biblical literature.

In a sense, the power to imagine in all areas of life is an intriguing human capacity, which can bring much joy, much fear, much helpful or harmful guidance.

35 / Individualism

In a speech class one term, when a student from Taiwan about thirty years old gave his speeches, the class expected him to speak about political issues involving Taiwan and the People's Republic of China. He was referred to as "that Chinese fellow." The identifying factor was his race and nationality.

Then the students learned that he was a physical education teacher, and they expected him to speak about sports, referring to him as "that phys ed teacher." By the end of the term, when he was mentioned, the classmates responded, "Oh, you mean Lee?" Like zooming in with a camera, the students came to identify him as an individual, not by his occupation or nationality. This growth in the students was a gratifying illustration of what all of us need to do, that is, to see people first and foremost as individuals.

Fingerprints identify our individuality, distinct from all other humans, like a snowflake that has no identical duplicate. We can recognize acquaintances on the phone by just their first word or two, for their voice has become unique to us. When a nagging parent admonishes an offspring to be like some other child, the frustrated boy or girl may well respond with profound wisdom: "But if I'll be like her/him, who will be like me?" Parents need to realize each child is different; teachers must recognize each student is an individual.

Western societies stress the individual, whereas Asian and other cultures emphasize the group as paramount. Whatever the cultural habits, the bottom line still should honor the uniqueness and preciousness of individuality.

With the mind-boggling advent of cloning sheep comes the agonizing ethical question whether the cloning of humans would profoundly intrude on the sanctity and distinctness of human individuality.

36 / In-Take and Out-Let

At the small lake on which we have a summer cottage, the water level is maintained by being spring fed and by two main creeks draining water from nearby farm lands. From the lake the water flows into a small swamp, which in turn empties into a small river system, the Sunrise River, which flows eventually into the St. Croix River (part of the boundary between Minnesota and Wisconsin), which in turn reaches the Mississippi River, and on down to the Gulf of Mexico. What an exciting route and ultimate destination for that small body of water!

Healthy lakes need an in-put and out-let. The Dead Sea serves as a metaphor for a stagnated no-outlet body of water. Office desks that have an in-box and out-box depict the flow of work material and symbolize an active productive person.

In academia, much is made of "publish or perish." That is, a professor is expected to publish articles and books or suffer the consequences of no salary increases or even loss of job, certainly loss of prestige with colleagues. In a deeper sense, one needs to publish in order not to perish intellectually, for without the constant in-flow (research, reading, experimenting, etc.) and out-flow (books, articles, book reviews, convention papers, public lectures, etc.), that professor is much like a stagnant dead sea. To flood one's desk and office with much research data and other materials, but not to export it to a larger public in some manageable fashion is indeed an indication that the person is not fully producing according to professional expectations.

In all areas of life, we would do well to recognize the importance of the in-take and the out-flow process, much like inhaling and exhaling need to be combined.

37 / It's the Interior that Counts

In European cities and some of our older ones on the Atlantic seaboard, one is struck by the often drab exteriors to buildings and homes, only to discover that the interiors are exquisitely beautiful. We enter into a different world when we go through those doors, and we learn anew that it is the interior that really counts.

A four-year-old child has learned that it is what is inside the gift box that really matters. A beautifully wrapped package from Aunt Mabel may contain only another unexciting article of clothing, whereas a plain-looking parcel may be hiding a wonderful toy. Surely we should have the savvy of a four-year-old and realize that exteriors and interiors do not necessarily coincide in significance.

We remember the familiar admonition that we are not to judge a book by its cover, and a medieval adage cautioned that a cloak maketh not a monk. One learns at an early age that classy uniforms do not necessarily make good athletes, bands, or dance ensembles. Gorgeous facades to buildings are just that—facades.

Indeed, it is the interior of a person that counts. The content of one's character, the integrity of one's being, is what we ought to seek to honor and develop.

38 / Fragility of Intermediacy

Life presents us with many moments when we are moving from one context, one station, to another—moments of intermediacy. At those times we are usually filled with apprehension, tension, and intensity, hence their fragility. We are uncertain what the outcome will be:

a cook preparing some dish—from a raw to a cooked state

a student writing an assigned paper—from raw data to a final composition

a person trying to repair a broken object—from brokenness to wholeness

a person learning to play a musical instrument—from hesitant noise to melodic strains

a committee trying to hammer out a recommendation—from rambling ideas and data to a coherent proposition

athletes locked in competition—from specific acts to final resolution

participants during the courtship phase—from free individuality to a committed bond of oneness

diplomats and negotiators—from uncharted waters to an agreed upon course

During these fragile periods of intermediacy, of moving from point A to point B, the participants may well need aloneness, silence, respectfulness from others, in order to work through the uncertainty and tension to a successful conclusion.

The intense fragility does not rule out pleasure. The joy of courtship is worth the uncertainties. The satisfaction experienced by the successful cook, student, repair person, musician, athlete, committee, and negotiators is heightened by the very fragility experienced during the process of their undertaking.

May we develop the necessary poise and confidence to work through our fragile episodes of intermediacy to experience the great pleasure en route.

39 / Intoxication

We most often associate intoxication with alcoholic beverages, whereby a person is led into various states ranging from exhilaration and uncontrolled motions to a dulling of the senses and even passing out. One's reasoning capacity and the ability to make moral judgments are radically impaired. One has literally abdicated one's independence, for one's ability to think, move, act, and judge has been relegated to others. A strong Declaration of Independence is needed. Coming from a Latin term meaning to put poison in, "intoxication" is indeed a poisoning of our being, or our humanity.

Driving cars and even boats when intoxicated results in untold deaths and injuries and legal penalties. Intoxication from drugs brings heart-wrenching personal and societal problems. But one can also say that intoxication with power and prestige leads many to push all potential competitors over the cliff with little remorse. Intoxication with the desire for peer acceptance, with plaudits from the crowd or our supervisors, may lead to unbalanced and unhealthy behavior. Intoxication with immediate sexual satisfaction has led to severe personal and societal damages.

But metaphorically, intoxication in the right things is a laudable state. An ancient sage asserted that one who is intoxicated with life has no need for wine. One could say that a person who is in love with life can hardly be drawn into the pits of drug and alcohol intoxication. Indeed, we need to be wise enough to become intoxicated with the right things.

40 / Journeying

The title of this book, *Along Life's Way*, employs the journey metaphor, dwelling on the image that life is indeed like a journey. We are depicted as continually going someplace. We may be characterized as wandering aimlessly or marching ahead with clear focus and discipline. Both portray the journey figure of speech.

The journey metaphor is often used in problem-solving rhetoric, as we speak of encountering "obstacles in our path" or stumbling along on a "rocky road." We are assured by candidates for public office that the obstacles will be removed and the bumpy pathway will be made smooth. They assure us they will "turn the country around," will set the nation in "a new direction." Dilemmas in public or personal life are depicted as "forks in the road," highlighting their uncertainties and their powerful potential to cause us to end up in vastly different destinations. We are reminded of the delicious bit of advice from Yogi Berra, who said, "When you come to a fork in the road, take it."

Politics, religion, business, sports, family life, and indeed all facets of life think regularly in the imagery of journeying. Most religions even carry the metaphor into some kind of afterlife, business is focused on the quarterly and annual earnings destinations, sports move through a given schedule toward the final standings. Parents keep admonishing their children to make wise decisions, to "go in the right direction."

Our reasoning process is depicted in a journey visualization. We "move" from facts to claims, we "arrive at" conclusions. Strong arguments "drive" us to a specific conclusion. We are engaged in a "step-by-step" process, we move from point A to point B, there is a destination to our mental meanderings.

41 / Finding the Kernel

Many people are reluctant to spend time in prolonged and intensive reading of the Bible or other religious or secular inspirational literature. It seems to be not worth the effort. We feel it is too lengthy, too repetitious, and too unimpressive, too unrealistic, too dogmatic, and too mystical. Too much chaff, we say. This understandable but unfortunate attitude keeps us from the excitement of encountering inspiring passages that bring to our lives challenge and comfort, direction and discipline, faith and freedom.

We might compare it to

discovering an exquisite porcelain vase at the bottom of a box filled with endless stuffing,
pushing aside the dense Cambodian jungle and coming onto the breathtaking wonders of Angkor Wat,
struggling in a desperately hot desert but eventually arriving at the coolness and beauty of an oasis,
listening to a lengthy, boring lecture, but suddenly being challenged by an arresting phrase which deepens our insights,
piercing the fuzzy darkness with a penetrating flashlight beam.

We ought not to acquiesce in the stuffing, jungle, desert, dry lecture, or darkness, but we ought to search patiently for the kernel. Untold exciting discoveries and beautiful opportunities have gone unclaimed by our unwillingness to sift through the chaff.

It may indeed be the stuffing that makes the vase seem even more beautiful, the jungle that makes the ancient ruins so breathtaking, the desert that makes the oasis so refreshing, the boredom that sets up the challenging insight, the darkness that makes the beam of light even more penetrating. Indeed, it may be the chaff that makes the kernel so nourishing.

42 / Leisure

Leisure activities are increasingly important to gain re-freshment in body and mind and spirit. Students look forward to the leisure time between terms. Parents savor the leisure when their children are away at the grandparents. Frantic-paced jobs drive many into expensive health clubs. Japan, where males work abnormally long hours at their business duties, is now intentionally trying to cut back on work expectations so that families can have more leisure time together. "Leisure studies" is a respected academic area of study, to help people learn lifetime sports and other activities that can be carried on into later years of life.

Then there is "forced leisure," that which is thrust upon the ill, the unemployed, the aged, the defeated political candidate, the exiled, the imprisoned. History is full of individuals who used such involuntary leisure to produce some great literature: Thucydides (5th century B.C.E.), Maimonides (12th century A.D.), Erasmus, Martin Luther, George Fox, and John Bunyan. Twentieth-century examples are Jawaharlal Nehru, Anwar Sadat, and Martin Luther King, Jr. Being retired from government duties enabled Nicolo Machiavelli (1496–1527) to do most of his writing, and ex-presidents and defeated candidates pen their memoirs. Unfortunately, some use leisure time in ways that are destructive to themselves and to society in general.

In one sense, time spent in school is leisure time; in fact, the term "school" means leisure. Children and young adults are excused from laboring in the fields, in the factories, in home, in the community, and instead are permitted to retreat to the quiet classroom.

How well do we use the leisure time, forced or free, we encounter in life? How well do we train ourselves in a multitude of healthy interests and activities carrying us on into the sunset of life?

43 / Libraries

As a youngster growing up during the Depression, I had few books in the home. I felt very proud when in woodworking class in high school I built my first bookcase—my library—which had two shelves, each less than two feet long, which I still possess.

It was really only in college and beyond that I vigorously "took off" in my reading habits and came to treasure libraries (and archives) as a central core of my work and enjoyment and veritable being.

What is a library? Coming from the Latin *liber*, it is essentially a repository of books—and of course many other things today. Only in the twentieth century have we moved away from the idea that libraries were basically storage places, with their contents under lock and key, with only designated personnel being permitted to work with the treasured holdings. The radical American concept of "open stacks," where students can retrieve their desired books themselves is gradually being adopted around the world. Libraries are where one life span can speak to another generation, where we can converse with the dead, where ideas compressed tightly on pages are set free to enter into our consciousness.

The inscription above the entrance to the famous Bodlieian Library in Oxford University says, when translated from the Latin: "Dedicated to the Republic of the Learned." Indeed, to those who are literate, books and libraries bring an egalitarianism, create a citizenry where all are equal.

Now that my wife and I are both retired from our professorships, our huge personal library has to be downsized, and perhaps I'll someday return to my two two-foot-long book shelves! It has been a glorious journey to spend one's life studying in libraries and archives around the world, mining information, generating ideas, and composing books and articles for those who will follow.

44 / Love

It has been said that the greatest tragedy in life is not to have loved and not to have been loved. Some wit has said that love is when two people see through each other and aren't bothered by the view! A contemporary ballad romantically asks, "What is this thing called love?" On a deeper level, humankind has perhaps forever been asking that same question.

A summary of love's dimensions, included in Paul's first letter to the Corinthians, chapter 13, has stood the test of centuries and still is the centerpiece for marriage ceremonies today: "Love suffereth long, and is kind; love envieth not; love vaunteth not itself, is not puffed up, doth not behave itself unseemly, seeketh not its own, is not provoked, taketh not account of evil; rejoiceth with the truth." At the end of the nineteenth century, a highly popular Scottish public speaker, Henry Drummond, in his off-repeated lecture, "The Greatest Thing in the World," reached thousands with his fuller development of Paul's characterization of love.

Martin Luther King, Jr. (1967) once expressed the difference between loving and liking in this way: "I can't like anybody who would trample over me with injustices. . . . I can't like anybody who threatens to kill me day in and day out. But Jesus reminds us that love is greater than liking. Love is understanding, creative, redemptive goodwill toward all men."

We love not only people, but we also assert that we love our work, we love certain foods, we love mountains and sunsets, we love activities like golf or baseball, we love our pets. Tagore (1961), the twentieth-century literary giant of India, spoke of love in this way: "Love gives beauty to everything it touches."

45 / Maintenance

We are far too slow to live up to long-range commitment inherent in appropriate maintenance.

Many individuals love to purchase new clothing, tools, and various other items, but they are inattentive to maintaining them with care. Governmental bodies love to build roads and bridges but are slow to allocate funding to keep them in good repair. Inadequate maintenance of school buildings in communities large and small result in dismal decay far before they should become aged.

Some nations and cultures pay close attention to maintenance, keeping things in good working order, whereas others tend to ignore investing time, thought, and concern in maintenance. In a number of developing countries, machinery stands idle in fields for lack of maintenance skills and resources.

Maintenance personnel in condominiums and other housing complexes are extremely important, not only in keeping the buildings and grounds in good repair, but in keeping the intangible richness of life at a high level. To have the long-range commitment and service of expert maintenance personnel is indeed a valuable asset.

The growing number of HMOs—health maintenance organizations—is testimony to the desire and wisdom of seeking to maintain good health in addition to repairing ill health.

Public parks, golf courses, tennis courts, and other recreational facilities fulfill their highest potential only when properly maintained. It is indeed sad to witness excellent facilities quickly lose appeal and function due to neglect.

46 / Mating

When I was a little boy growing up in a small Minnesota town near a lake, we would play various games digging in the sand, and we had the expression, "If you dig deeply enough, you'll come to China." Little did I know that at that very moment, southwest of China, in Burma (Myanmar), a little girl about my age was also digging in the sand.

And we met. Not in the center of the earth, but in Minneapolis, on the University of Minnesota campus. She was a graduate student at the University of Wisconsin, Madison, spending the summer in Minneapolis on a student work-study project, and living with her group in a fraternity house. We first met as participants on a panel discussion, when by chance I agreed to replace a friend of mine who was supposed to chair the panel.

That "intellectual" beginning resulted in a wedding in Madison three years later. Through these now forty-six years of a wonderfully happy and enriching international, intercultural marriage, we have been deeply blessed, and one realizes more fully as each year rolls by how very fortunate one is in this life to "find" the perfect mate, one's soul mate. As the musical admonishes us, "once you have found her, never let her go."

Through these many decades until our recent retirements, I taught Speech Communication at the University of Minnesota, and she was a Professor of Asian and European History at nearby Augsburg College. She fulfilled with excellence and with grace her multiple roles of professor, wife, mother (of a son and daughter), grandmother of five lovely grandchildren, and as a national and international leader in her church work.

How very proud I am of her, and how deeply grateful I am for having "found" her!

47 / Meditation

Most religions and other contemplative groups and individuals laud the practice of meditation, and some place it at the core of their lives. Many religious institutions emphasize retreats of short or long duration to reflect on one's goals and beliefs, one's short-comings ad general behavior. Some with strong mystical leanings, like Taoism and Buddhism, have placed an unusual stress on meditative exercises, whereas the more pragmatic Confucius was not very impressed: "I once spent a whole day without food and a whole night without sleep, in order to meditate. It was no use. It is better to learn" (19:30).

But learning and meditating are not necessarily mutually exclusive; in fact, they usually do, or should, go together. Daily meditation in our hectic modern scientific age is extremely important. Reading devotional, inspirational, or philosophical literature, coupled with a brief period of silence, perhaps at a set time of day, can be immensely rewarding in contributing to spiritual and intellectual growth, in calming tensions, and in setting and maintaining directions in life. Augustine long ago suggested: "Let set times be appointed, and certain hours be ordered for the health of our soul." To maintain a regular linkage with that which is behind and throughout all of life gives one a healthy, long-range view of existence.

To engage in such a set habit of meditation together with a loved one, present or in some other locality, can be extremely meaningful. For instance, when my wife and I were courting for over two years in our graduate school days, our universities were hundreds of miles apart, but some of the most treasured thirty minutes of each day were when at 10:00 P.M. each would stop to read his or her chosen devotional literature. A deep sense of being at one with each other was experienced. Furthermore, it is amazing how many books one will read in a year's time, which otherwise probably would not have been explored!

48 / Memory

The gift of memory is an awesome dimension to our lives. To bring to the forefront of our consciousness some happy event in the near or distant past is indeed a blessing of immeasurable worth. Conversely, the recall of bad memories can plague us unrelentingly even to the end of our life.

Some frightful historical events, such as the Holocaust, need to be vigorously remembered to lessen the likelihood of such subhuman atrocities occurring in the future. Conversely, ethnic, tribal, religious, and national relationships might be greatly enriched if their historical memories of past atrocities were forgotten, such as the Irish and the English, Israelis and Arabs, Serbs and Croats, etc.

Family memories likewise can be full of happiness or sadness. We marvel and rejoice at the details children remember from conversations and family activities of long ago. We build family memories from vacation trips and other special traditions. We record our family memories in our photo albums, video footage, and written histories. How precious these are, even sad memories, to those in the family circle.

Businesses, educational and religious institutions, fraternities and sororities, sports clubs, and many other organizations give much attention to retaining and passing on historical memories of their associations. People purchase old objects at garage sales and auctions for the sake of sentimental memories. At the auction of Jackie Kennedy's possessions, astronomical sums were spent by those who viewed their seemingly reckless acts as buying historical memories.

Computers and robots now make fun of us humans by possessing elaborate memory banks. Alzheimer's and other diseases of

51

the elderly rob us of our memory bank deposits. How tragic to lose such an integral part of our being!

We need to value the gift of memory as long as we possess it, and to be glad.

49 / Middle-of-the-Road

In the democratic political process, pragmatic leaders know they have to carve out a middle-of-the-road position to be elected and to push legislation through divided legislative bodies. Sometimes those people are hailed as skillful compromisers, mature public servants who know how to get things done for the benefit of the general society. Sometimes those people are chastised as people of no firm principle, who, bending with the winds of current opinion, modify their stance with ease.

The Golden Mean, the thoughtful middle, the avoiding of extreme polar positions, has been praised by and been identified with such ancient intellectual heavyweights of the West and East as Aristotle and Confucius. It has, however, been said by some wit that people in the middle-of-the-road will probably get run over. It has also been noted that persons sometimes may hold moderate views in an immoderate manner, that is, being too ready to label those at the extremes as parochial, doctrinaire fanatics. With comparable danger, those holding to polar positions sometimes claim that extremism in the cause of some cherished value, such as liberty or freedom, is an unassailable virtue.

What we search for as individuals and as a society is a "comfort zone" between extremes, where people of varying persuasions can live in reasonable harmony in the broad middle ground, holding to undergirding values but accommodating to people who lean in different directions.

50 / What's on Your Mind?

On a continuum stretching from an easy conversation opener to a probing, open-ended query of a psychiatrist, the question, "What's on your mind?" reaches to the very core of our being. We are what is on our minds.

"Think on these things," ancient literature admonishes us, followed by a list of commendable values. We know that if we indeed focus on worthwhile entities, our lives are strengthened and we enrich the lives of those around us.

Sometimes we feel depressed and guilty that we harbor weird and even hurtful thoughts, which uninvitedly flit into our consciousness. It may be unfair to chastise ourselves too much or brood about it, for it is like a bat getting into our house. We didn't invite it, but there it is, generating great consternation and effort to get rid of it. Our guilt ought not to be too heavy, for who can completely control the portals to one's mind?

Some thoughts just won't go away. They linger and linger, gnawing away at our sense of well-being. Sometimes thoughts demanding some action can be eliminated by allocating specific time to them. For example, a household job that has been "on our mind" for weeks suddenly melts away after we fix that sluggish drain or rearrange that unsightly closet. We often are pleasantly surprised that the task took as little time to accomplish as it did, and we wonder why we didn't get it "off" our mind earlier.

Paradoxically, it often helps to get things "off" our mind by putting more on it, for thus no one worry looms too large. Each becomes more appropriately a mere pebble on the beach rather than one big boulder. Retirees and others often suffer from having too little on their minds, and thus little worries become magnified.

We need to take periodic inventory as to what we have "on our minds," and to develop a healthy reaction to those inhabitants.

51 / Mountains

Mountains have served humankind for centuries both as a challenging physical phenomenon and as a metaphorical source of strength and solace. From the ancient Hebrew proclamation, "from whence cometh my help," to *The Sound of Music*'s "I go to the hills, when my heart is lonely," this universal pull to the heights is acknowledged.

We are energized by the sight of the United States and Canadian Rockies and the Swiss Alps, and are positively overwhelmed by the awesome Himalayas. We speak of "mountaintop"experiences in life. The heights give a soul-cleansing, long-range vision, a bracing wind, and a sense of proportion to one's inner worries. Skiers and mountain bikers and hikers would quickly add that the heights also give the refreshment of vigorous exercise and the excitement of sights seen from new vantage points, and of the sense of accomplishment to have gone where few have gone. Mountain climbers for centuries have sought to scale the beckoning peaks simply because "they are there."

Mountains have served as a source of wisdom and spiritual insight, so it is understandable that Moses received the Ten Commandments upon Mount Sinai, or that Christian, Taoist, and Buddhist monasteries are usually found in mountain hideaways. Hawaii's goddess "Pele" resides in the volcanic heights, not on Waikiki Beach.

Some financial institutions, such as insurance companies, have mountains as their logo to symbolize security and stability. Statesmen, particularly in times of crises, often make emotional appeals to mountain images. For instance, David Lloyd George (1914), British Prime Minister during World War I, spoke colorfully of his beloved Welsh mountains, symbolizing honor and strength and country: a "great pinnacle of sacrifice pointing like a rugged finger to Heaven . . . these great mountain peaks, whose foundations are unshaken though Europe rock and sway in the convulsions of a great war."

52 / Movement

The staccato bark of the army sergeant of "move it, move it, move it," to get the recruits to hustle, can be symbolic of much of life. Businesses seek to stack their shelves only with products that will "move." A football team is obsessed with moving the ball downfield. Checkers and chess are centrally concerned with good "moves." In schooling and other training contexts, we are focused on moving along from one level of proficiency to the next. The eternal pleasure of being on a river is that it persistently moves us along, even if ever so slowly.

In the social, political, religious, and other areas of life, there often emerge "movements," which seek to direct thought and energy and structure to certain ends. The civil rights movement and the feminist movement have left their indelible marks on society. In academia, "movement studies" are a significant genre of research in such disciplines as sociology, political science, and communication. We harbor the image that not to "move" is to stagnate, to preserve a status quo that more than likely does not deserve to remain.

Political figures campaigning for public office like to emphasize in what directions they would supposedly "move" the nation if elected. Negotiators announce that their sessions with two factions were showing "movement" toward eventual resolution. Indeed, in most areas of life, we define our activities and hopes in terms of movement.

The question is, do the destinations merit our effort and commitment?

53 / Multiple-ness

We need to realize more fully that most of life's situations are composed of multiple strands. More than one cause is operating to produce a particular effect. More than one motive is pushing us to make an important decision. We tend to look for *the* reason for something, as if there is only *one*. We ought not to succumb to this folly of oneness, this sin of singularity.

In answer to what are we going to do with our life, we may well respond with multiple possibilities, especially in today's fluid economic conditions and institutional downsizing. Former generations usually thought of preparing for only one occupation, which, while it had the laudatory feature of focus, now increasingly has the misleading emphasis that there is only one path we can or ought to pursue.

A liberal arts education is seen today by many as being even more important, for it strengthens a person in many different directions, thus fortifying oneself for different kinds of employment and making one a more appealing candidate for job opportunities.

With the world getting smaller, with the world's population moving dramatically because of war and famine, because of the search for new opportunities, many countries, and surely the United States, are experiencing a multiethnic, multiracial mix of people. The need to live more intelligently and compassionately in multicultural surroundings is a challenge, which will only grow in intensity and significance as we enter the twenty-first century. Those who are comfortable only among their narrow tribal, ethnic, or religious compatriots will need to broaden their horizons or be left behind in parochial ghettos, missing out on the rich experience of life's multiple offerings.

To appreciate the multiple components of a mosaic, of a woven tapestry, of a rainbow, is to drink in a refreshing dimension of life.

58

54 / Naming

Small children give names to their dolls, stuffed animals, and toys. Adults name their cars and boats. Suddenly those "things" come alive and share in the human dimension. What a swift and glorious transformation! Perhaps it's comparable to the biblical narrative of the Creator giving names to the dust of the earth, thus "creating" human beings?

Names for the "Creator"—Jehovah, God, Allah, Father, Mother, Supreme Being—for some people establishes a comforting sense of linkage with the awesome power behind all of life, but alienates others who find such naming irrational and simplistic.

We somehow feel better when the doctor gives a name to our illness, unless of course the label is a fearful one, like "cancer." Attaching a label to someone may construct a rigid and unfair stereotype—a "troublemaker," a "shyster," a "couch potato." Such name-calling may well exaggerate an aspect of another person's character and probably overlooks other dimensions. When a new neighbor moved next door to us, their large dog at first seemed rather menacing, but when we learned her name, she suddenly became a gentle pet. Such is the power of language, of naming.

Another twist is that we can know certain people by their names for years, such as the authors of textbooks, but when we meet them in person, at a conference for example, we "see" them in a new light. Putting a face on names is an intriguing dynamic, sometimes raising, sometimes lowering, sometimes confirming, sometimes disconfirming, our original estimation.

To name is to link us more closely with life around us, and to name wisely is merely another specific way to live wisely.

55 / Through Negatives to Positives

Experiencing negative situations often leads us into a fuller and richer appreciation for the positives in life:

by the loneliness of separation, one basks in the fulfillment of to-
    getherness,
by the high cost of ignorance, one sees the relatively low cost of
    education,
by the weakness of falsity is the strength of truth demonstrated,
by the bad news in a speech, the concluding optimism soars even
    higher,
by the ugliness of the unkempt is the beauty of tidiness seen,
by the suffering of pain, one feels the relief of its absence,
by the paralysis of fear, one rejoices in its dissipation,
by the unattractiveness of the unpainted is the beauty of the
    painted appreciated,
by the roughness of the wood is the smoothness of the sanded
    product felt,
by ill health is good health savored,
by the loss of freedom is its acquisition celebrated,
by the cruelty of the villain is the kindness of the hero appreci-
    ated,
by the harshness of the tyrant, one feels the balm of the liberator,
by the arrogance of the bigot, one appreciates the mellowness of
    the openminded,
by the ignorance of one's peers is one's own relative intelligence
    perceived,
by the heat of the day, the coolness of the evening is felt,
by the darkness of the night is the brightness of the day seen.

But surely one shouldn't necessarily have to experience the negatives in order to "latch on to the affirmatives," for one need not walk into quicksand in order to appreciate firm ground.

56 / Nineteenth Hole

Following eighteen holes of golf, it's traditional to relax in the clubhouse or a nearby restaurant for refreshments, good-humored banter about the game just completed, and maybe serious analysis of mistakes in hopes of doing better next time. Idle chatter and good fellowship increase the pleasure of the outing and provide a "long view" of things after the tensions of the game just completed. It's a chance to savor one's good performances and to commiserate over unfortunate "unlucky" shots.

Occasionally the discussion may turn to more serious topics, such as one's problems at work or home, one's health concerns, one's social relationships, or one's plans for the future. The nineteenth hole, then, can generate important healing, stimulating ideas, and helpful guidance.

Similar experiences occur at "happy hours" at the end of a day or a week, and many bars and restaurants capitalize on this desire in humans. We have to earn these happy hours, however, hence they occur after a day's efforts, not before, after a week's accomplishments, not on Mondays.

Other situations resemble the nineteenth hole. "Receptions" following some event, such as graduations, concerts, special lectures, or church services, encourage informal conversation among the audience members, with some of the above potential benefits.

Life can be enriched significantly by such nineteenth-hole opportunities, permitting people to interact on an informal basis after the completion of some task, large or small.

57 / Oakkhin

Our cottage property, located on a small country lake a short distance from our Twin Cities home, is dominated by seven huge, rugged oak trees. My wife's Burmese name is Khin Khin (pronounced "kin"), hence we named our lake home "Oakkhin," Oak + Khin.

A chance phonetic factor contributed to the choice of name. Khin Khin's family lived in a lovely suburban area of the Burmese capital, Rangoon (now Yangon), which was badly bombed by the Americans in 1944 as they drove out the occupying Japanese forces. The name of her residence was "Okkyin" (pronounced "o kin"), hence the phonetic similarity. It seemed to be appropriate as a sort of replacement of a loss sustained by American action to have Khin Khin's American home carry a name reminiscent of her origins.

But the meaningfulness of Oakkhin goes beyond just the name, for like many lake homes, it has provided, for three decades, a place of refuge from the responsibilities of our urban work and rush, a place to unwind, to reflect on life. It has enabled us to get the long view, to sort out the important, the less important, and the unimportant. Swimming, water skiing, canoeing, boating, fishing, and pontoon-ing have had their input to our enjoyment to varying degrees and at varying times in our family history. Walking around the lake, observing the cycles of growth of nature and farm fields through spring, summer, and fall, and reading during inclement weather have enriched our lives.

The labor needed in the upkeep, while often time-consuming and exhausting, also has been a helpful component in relaxing. Lawn-mowing, weed and brush control, care of flowers, dock and boat and house maintenance indeed often served to heal the soul. To "get away" is an important part of life's journey, and we are grateful for Oakkhin's ministry to us through the years.

58 / Oldness

When does one become "old"? Obviously it is relative to many things. If one is blessed with good health, one may look and feel "young" despite a high chronological number. We seek to grow old without getting "old," to remain young in body, spirit, and mind. We seek various fountains of youth and in various ways. The American culture honors youth, whereas others honor age.

Today people are living much longer than they were a century ago. Most cultures have a built-in desire to respect and treat well the aged among them, but that manifests itself in different ways. In the United States, we look positively on special homes for the elderly, whereas other cultures would consider it disrespectful to move the elderly out of the family home.

Fortunately, there are many lighthearted witticisms about growing old, which help to soften any sadness that might be present:

"Now that we know all the answers, no one is asking us any questions."

"Aches and pains are one's body's way of telling us something—and as we get older, our body gets more talkative."

"It's better to be over the hill than under it."

"If I had known I would live so long, I would have taken care of myself."

The golfer Patty Berg at the age of seventy-four: "I'm not old, I'm only two over par."

When we grow old, we somehow seem more stupid; not that we are, but we just lose the ability to hide it.

"Old university deans never die, they just lose their faculties."

Being seventy is the perfect time to learn to play a musical instrument, for one has enough time to practice but not enough time to worry about getting good.

One dreads getting old, for one thinks one will be unable to do the things one likes to do, but when one gets old, one discovers one no longer wants to do them.

59 / Being #1

Many people, by nature and/or by socialization, possess a driving desire to be "number one." Students seek to be at the top of their class, athletes hope to be selected their team's most valuable player, business persons eye the top of the corporate ladder. In Olympic competition, many participants and observers feel that being less than #1 is somehow a failure. Nations marshall their efforts to be #1 economically and militarily. Educational institutions seek to be ranked #1. Politicians settle only for the top position.

We applaud this desire to use talents and resources to the highest degree possible. But we also lament the blind obsession that often accompanies the desire to be #1. A student cheats to get the highest grade, an athlete pushes others aside, a business person steps on anyone who gets in the way, nations run roughshod over rivals, educational institutions exaggerate their strengths, and politicians demean others in the area. Do we push aside and hurt others in our scramble to the top? Do we neglect loved ones in our race for the prize? What is the price tag on our victory?

A touch of Taoism might be healthy, for one of its three central precepts is the blunt admonition, "do not seek to be number one." Of course that can lead to an obsession with inaction, with minimal effort, with undeveloped talents. Obviously some balance is needed.

One needs to revel in the excitement of striving to be the best one can possibly be, but yet realize that the full and satisfying life does not demand to be #1. Some wit has observed that mediocrity is okay, as long as you are good at it!

60 / Through Open Windows and Doors

I have a vivid memory of childhood years, when our next-door neighbor, Mrs. Olson, a kindly, efficient Swedish housewife, would bake bread, rolls, cookies, cakes, and pies, and in the summer, the tantalizing odor would reach me through her open doors and windows. The odor was even more pleasant because I could expect her to invite me to sample her freshly baked goodies.

Through those same open doors and windows in a subsequent summer, came the desperate and agonizing screams and groans of Mrs. Olson, painfully suffering from stomach cancer, silenced only temporarily and periodically by hypo injections and eventually, permanently by death. It caused me to reflect that my first two months of life on this earth were my father's last two months, as he too went through an agonizing death from stomach cancer.

How true it is that through the same open doors and windows of life can come the deepest joys and the most agonizing pains:

the joy of a perfect marriage, or the agony of a wrenching divorce;
the joy of children grown to lovely adulthood, or trying to cope with dangerously anti-social offspring;
a job bringing initial fulfillment and challenge, only to bring daily stress and no future;
public parks once a pleasant environment for all ages, declining into dangerous hang-outs for society's trouble-makers;
nationalism bringing unity and safety to tribes and provinces, but producing weaponry that brings even greater fear and insecurity to all.

The neutrality of open doors and windows—conduits of both joy and grief—is indeed part of life's reality.

61 / Overlays

Human speech is defined as an overlaid function. The lungs, larynx, nasal passage, teeth, lips, alveolar ridge, and uvula are primarily utilized for the life-preserving functions of breathing and eating, and only secondarily employed for speaking.

Psychologically, we benefit from overlays of problems, as strange as that may seem. We carry a concern about a particular problem in our head, and what often relieves us is not the elimination of that problem but the appearance of a new problem, which overlays and actually diminishes our anxiety of the first one. The death of a friend suddenly makes other problems seem very insignificant; they don't go away, but are overlaid by a greater remorse. By the time we get back to those initial worries, their intensity is considerably lessened.

Religion employs overlays. A chosen small boy is revered in Buddhism, believed to be the reincarnated spirit of a previous renowned Buddha figure, and he is given attendants and tutors and granted great deference. Watching him run and act like any other boy his age makes it difficult to see this overlay of veneration, unless you are a believer. The Papacy in Roman Catholicism and hierarchical leaders throughout Christianity, Judaism, Islam, as well as other religions overlay themselves with garb and claims of spiritual power and significance.

Politics also employs overlays. Even today royal families are granted, or usurp, enormous residences, elegant surroundings, huge estates, great wealth, and considerable power, all in the name of providing through their beings a sense of overlaid unity to a given nation. Ancient monarchs in the Mediterranean area took on the names and claimed the overlaid qualities of mythical deities. National flags and anthems provide an overlaid umbrella of national oneness and cohesion.

62 / People Problems

One might summarize and categorize the "people problems" of the twenty-first century yearning to be solved as the following, realizing how incomplete is the list and the few examples given:

1. begetting people (population controls, abortion, surrogate parents)
2. feeding people (food production and distribution, soil and water management, marketing, trade policies and practices, deep sea exploration)
3. protecting people (crime control, national defense, weapon proliferation from hand guns to atomic bombs, responsible use of policing powers, space exploration)
4. employing people (unemployment, underemployment, part-time employment, job security, work safety and satisfaction, parental leaves, nursery facilities)
5. healing people (health-care facilities, cost, distribution, insurance, research)
6. moving people (transportation facilities and safety, immigration, refugees)
7. educating people (pre-school through graduate school, professions, trades, high tech, liberal arts, life-long learning)
8. nurturing people (blending independence with a sense of community, leadership development, moral maturity)
9. integrating people (multicultural interaction, bilingualism, equality of opportunity)
10. informing people (telephone, fax, visual, electronic, satellite, print, computers, cellular, interpersonal, small groups, public discourse)
11. sheltering people (single-family and condo housing, environment, air pollution)

12. re-creating people (leisure time use, lifetime sports, park systems, wilderness preservation, artistic and musical performances, entertainment via stage and television)

63 / Perfection

Surely one of the central life-affirming values is the striving for excellence, the pursuit of perfection. But is there a limit to perfection? Can it even lead to debasement?

What of the "perfected" combination of science, industry, and military to make horrendous weaponry at enormous cost and in the end creating new dangers? To what end is the "perfection" of smartly goose-stepping soldiers on parade? How devastating it is to see the perfected grace and precision displayed in athletic contests be turned to cruel behavior in other situations. How important is it to have enormously expensive, complicated equipment to strengthen a few muscles in a few athletes and a few other individuals?

How about the "perfection" of grand religious architecture, which submerges the humble essence of the worship experience? There is a sad irony in the Taj Mahals of this world—perfect in form and beauty, but speaking to one man's sorrow and vanity, while thousands live in abject poverty around it.

How about higher education, which trumpets its "passion for excellence" but deemphasizes such mundane things as conscientious teaching and empathic advising? How about carefully honed business procedures and advertising techniques that make and sell unnecessary and even dangerous products to people? Once we have achieved perfection in convenience, speed, and comfort, what then?

In our legitimate striving for perfection, we may well need to ask if there are some boundaries, some limits, beyond which it is unwise to go. Surely we must ever ask ourselves to what end is the perfection directed.

64 / Pets

Returning from work, where people treat you like dog, to home where your dog treats you like royalty sums up one important dimension of the value of pets! They release our tensions with their unconditional attention and affection.

President Truman advised people that if they were looking for a friend in the politically charged atmosphere of Washington, D.C., they would be better off buying a dog!

Pets comfort and entertain us, and they serve as playmates. A small child romping with its dog is an endearing sight of mutual happiness. Our family for over thirteen years owned a lovable little pekapoo, "Pebbles," part Pekingese and part poodle, and she greatly enriched our lives.

Scholarly studies have documented what humans have known for centuries—that pets are good for people. For the elderly, for single people, for shut-ins, for the physically and mentally disabled, pets are especially precious life-enhancing companions. A cat in the lap, a dog by your side, a bird singing in a cage, goldfish swimming in the fishbowl—what intangible blessings!

A loudly barking dog (often with a friendly wagging tail!) frightens away intruders, and owners feel safer. People feel a sense of accomplishment by being in complete (usually!) control of their companions.

There are some potential negatives, of course. Children have long wearied parents with pets not in the mainstream—lizards, frogs, turtles, raccoons, snakes, etc. Some adults with their unusual and/or uncontrolled pets have alienated neighbors. Feeding and medical costs for some pets can be sizable, and "we've got to get home to let the dog out" can restrict one's freedom of activity.

But we rejoice in that wonderful entangling alliance between pets and humans!

65 / Place

Humans are attached to land, to country, to place. A scholar of geography, Yi-Fu Tuan, calls this love of place "topophila."

Some nations or tribes assert that "their" land was granted to them by some deity, as if the Creator of the universe was in the real estate business. Nations praise their geology and geography, as we in America eloquently sing of our "purple mountains majesties," "fruited plain," "rocks and rills" and "woods and templed hills." In time of war, most nations emotionally glorify their undertaking by speaking of protecting their "sacred soil." These "places," these geographical/geological reference points often generate a powerful rhetorical impact, which I choose to call "geo-rhetorica." Each nation also has its historic sites, its battlefields, its monuments, its special "places," which perpetuate memory and stimulate devotion.

To most religions, "place" is extremely important, be it a city (Jerusalem, Mecca, Rome), a river (Ganges), a mountain (Mount Sinai), etc., which often beckons believers to make a pilgrimage to them.

These "places" can unfortunately build an unhealthy inward-looking parochialism, a "holier than thou" attitude. John Haynes Holmes (1879–1964) warned: "From pride of place absolve" us and Lloyd Stone's "Hymn of All Nations" of the United Nations, sung to the tune of Sibelius's *Finlandia*, tries to expand our geo-rhetorical vistas:

> But other lands have sunlight too, and clover
> And skies are everywhere as blue as mine.
> O hear my song, Thou God of all the nations,
> A song of peace—for their land and for mine.

66 / Porches

Older and bigger houses of earlier times often included a large porch in the front, serving as a transition area before entering the house itself. With their pillars, these porches often were an attractive and prestigious mansionlike frontage.

Many porches included a swing fastened to the ceiling and other benches and chairs where people could on a summer evening sit and chat with family members and with neighbors or others passing by. Children played simple games, and courting couples savored goodnight kisses there. The porch was where meaningful and usually pleasant discussion occurred.

Some porches eventually became enclosed, and thus served as an extra room of the house. It was there that children would enjoy sleeping on warm summer nights, and the family would enjoy informal meals, making it a sort of halfway facility between the dining room and eating outside. If facing east, the porch caught the first warm rays of the morning sun and the cool shade of the evening; if facing west, it experienced morning coolness and afternoon warmth.

In my many years of teaching, what I metaphorically called "porch discussions" were very important. The "porch" was those few minutes immediately prior to and after a class period, a time when the instructor could engage in informal discussion with one or more students about classwork or anything that seemed to be of interest. This helped to establish and maintain a linkage between teacher and students that I felt was mutually rewarding.

In our busy lives, usually dashing from Point A to Point B, we need to take time to make ourselves open to "porch discussions," for, however brief, they can create vital and enriching linkages.

67 / Position

In doing tasks around the home, we learn the importance of first getting into the proper position. When doing that plumbing job under the sink, one first gets into a comfortable position to protect one's body and to do the repair more efficiently. We learn not to stretch awkwardly when reaching for something on a high shelf or reaching for garments in the back of the closet. When painting the house or some other building, we know the importance of being in the proper position on the ladder or scaffold, not to stretch so as to make conditions unsafe and increase the likelihood of doing a less than adequate job. Working in the garden or cutting weeds, we learn to protect our back by being in the proper position.

When writing at our desk, we get the arm up on the desk, to write more effectively and to avoid cramping our arm. When giving a public speech, we learn the importance of keeping both feet flat on the floor, to be in a firm and comfortable position to lessen our tension and improve our presentation.

Athletes learn of the importance of being in the right position in anticipation of doing their tasks effectively. A shortstop in baseball learns to position himself properly before making that long throw to first base. An outfielder shifts position to match the anticipated hitting habits of the batter.

Being in the right place at the right time and in the right position is critical in the effective accomplishment of life's tasks.

68 / Possessions

How is it that we come to "possess" things? We "buy" them with money or with some bartering arrangement. We acquire land by purchasing it from the previous owner, but how did that person come to "own" it? We trace the title deed of a house to determine former owners, but how did the original owner secure it? Religious and legal stipulations that "thou shalt not steal" assumes that people "own" things. They further imply that the "owner" acquired them through some appropriate means.

Throughout the world, powerful people, noblemen, and monarchs simply acquired land through force and power. Suppose a contemporary person asked a large land owner, "How did you come to own this land?"

"I inherited it from my family."

"But how did they acquire it?"

"From their parents."

"But how did your family first acquire the land?"

"My ancestor fought for it and defeated any rivals."

"Okay, then I'll fight you for it!"

Monarchs acquire enormous land holdings and dole out parcels to loyal families, thus entrenching control over the populace. Governments "buy" land from others who had probably acquired it through force in the first place.

Land reforms in various countries attempt to even out to some minor degree through legal means the huge disparity between the few very wealthy "owners" and the many very poor dispossessed.

We also "possess" intangibles, such as education, principle, knowledge, and skills. Wise admonitions for centuries have told us to focus on possessing those intangibles in life that "thieves can neither rob nor rust destroy."

69 / Power

Humans are motivated by many tempters, but none perhaps as omnipresent and strong as power. People will kill for it. Life becomes for many a constant scramble for it, from the baby who learns that boisterous crying will wield power over a parent, to children on the playground seeking to excel over their peers, to teenagers hungering for dominance in their circle of acquaintances, to the adult ladder-climbers, all the way to those who reach the pinnacle of success in their chosen paths.

Humans motivated by the desire for wealth are perhaps not as dangerous as people driven by the desire for power. The former are relatively more willing to be satisfied with a degree a wealth, whereas the latter continue to desire more and more power. Those who possess great wealth may actually voluntarily give some away through philanthropic or other informal channels, but those who possess great power seldom give any of it away, for it is more intangible and not so easily measured.

The power-hungry often seek not only to weaken opponents but to eliminate them. National hoarders of power in dictatorships demand complete allegiance to, and virtual worship of, those at the top of the hierarchy. Vaclav Havel (1992), now president of the Czech Republic, wrote caustically of the former Communist regime: "the wasteland of life in a totalitarian state, with its all-powerful center and all-powerless inhabitants" (p. 294).

Power and virtue are not parallel railroad tracks. Alive in the land is the strange notion that those who possess great power also possess great virtue. This is matched by the similarly strange notion that those who have no or little power somehow have great virtue.

When the power-ful share it with the power-less in society, great strides can be taken to create a healthy and enriched society.

70 / Preservation

What should we preserve? Individuals and institutions and society in general constantly have to contend with that question. When we move to another house, to another job, or into retirement, we wonder what is worth keeping. When children move into adult-hood, they and their parents wonder what belongings of child-hood could well be disposed of.

As educational institutions grow, they wonder what of their past in terms of buildings and curriculum should be saved. At a small college with which I am familiar, a few years ago, some fac-ulty and students picketed the administration's decision to tear down an old house resting on a central portion of the campus. The protesters emphasized the importance of keeping this historic structure, to help preserve the college's past. Fortunately, in this instance, the administration went ahead with their plans, and now in that strategic location stands an excellent student center building with numerous facilities, serving as an enormously func-tional and beautiful centerpiece. The pulsating soul of the college lives on more vigorously than it would have otherwise. To pre-serve buildings but deny the soul's development seems counter-productive. In other instances, of course, institutions are wise to keep and rehabilitate old structures for the sake of tangible histor-ical memories.

That institutions, communities, individuals, and nations should have sensitivity to preserving their past for the sake of fu-ture generations is indeed commendable. But when we do decide to preserve, let us be clear that it doesn't stand in the way of rea-sonable and sensible progress, and that values being honored are indeed worthy of such preservation.

71 / Questioning

Questioning is the springboard of scholarly research, wise policy making, and every man's progress. Without questions, new knowledge lies hidden, improved policies are still-born, and higher plateaus in life are never reached.

We all too soon seem to lose the probing spirit of a child's persistent "why?" Exhausted parents stifle it, and too few teachers encourage it. We need to retain that childlike urgency of wanting to push back the shrouds in search of an understanding of this strange world in which we live and move and have our being.

Occasionally when driving to a new destination, we may doubt that the suggested main thoroughfare is the best way and have a feeling of pride in our bold initiative to strike out on a different route. But after the passage of some miles, we may discover that we made a faulty choice and that a different way needs to be taken, even returning to the original main thoroughfare.

Many "doubters" accept blindly their first detour and do not question their questioning. They become "true believers" in their detour, while ridiculing those who remain on the main thoroughfare. One needs to doubt one's doubts, question one's questioning. Not to continue questioning simply leads one into forming new ruts, as confining as the original road. One also needs to question one's second and third turn-offs and should at least keep as an option the original main thoroughfare.

It takes a strength of mind and character to accept that in our questioning we may never "arrive," but are forever questing. The journey of life may have many varied routes ahead of us, and the uncertainty that comes with questioning also brings a freshness and verve and excellence to life's choices and conclusions.

72 / Reading

To be able to read is to open up endless horizons to our life. Thus, most societies place a primary emphasis on literacy, at least a rudimentary level. School systems are judged by the degree of reading proficiency of their students, and the more advanced societies are forever trying to improve that proficiency. Not to be able to read brings untold handicaps and lack of opportunities for the individual and a weakening of the tissue of society.

Small children love the world of books, of having people read to them, of eventually being able to read for themselves. For many adults, too, "curling up with a book" is a pleasure much treasured. In our electronic age, it is feared by some that people will no longer immerse themselves in book reading, preferring the passive absorption of television or surfing on the internet. But research and experience suggests otherwise. Watching on television the portrayal of a novel, rather than lessening the chances of people reading the book, is more likely to lead more readers to it and to other literature (Kantar, 1990).

Many signs are present indicating the growth rather than the decline in reading. Numerous book clubs are springing up, in private homes, religious and educational institutions, and residential complexes. The phenomenal success of Oprah Winfrey's book-club innovation shows the hunger for, and willingness to engage in, book reading in the general populace. Bookstore sales are prospering, and the growing inclusion of bookstore café corners draws on and fosters the love of casual lounging with a book as a companion.

We read to stretch our minds, our experiences, and our knowledge. We read to escape from, but also to become more involved in, life around us. What we are reading defines in large measure who and what we are.

73 / Retirement

Retirement can be a mixed bag. For many it is a wonderful release from crushing daily obligations, an entry into a land of freedom and flexibility. To others, it brings an aimless existence, a sense of being lost, of not knowing what to do with one's time. It obviously is crucial to have interests, old or new, to pursue, and to have friends, old or new, with whom to interact. Some retirees have family close by, but others do not; some lose contact with former colleagues, but some keep in touch. Some retirees are financially secure, but others are not.

One feature that can be obnoxious is that peripheral tasks edge their way to center stage. Shopping for groceries, for example, which one used to fit in sometime between the cracks of a busy schedule, now becomes *the* significant accomplishment of the day. Little tasks boldly claim the chief seats at the table.

Wisdom from the ages speaks to retirement. The writer of Ecclesiastes (2:18–19) touches on the realistic concern of who will carry on our work in our place: "I must leave it [my labor] unto the man that shall be after me. And who knoweth whether he will be a wise man or a fool?" Unwisely putting off retirement was warned against by Chuang Tzu, a powerful Chinese warlord, who added to his success by conquering city after city and couldn't resist taking someone's advice that he try to conquer the desert. That was his downfall: "He could not bring himself to retire. He had forgotten how to stop his wagon" (Merton, 1959). How many contemporary CEOs, professors, and government officials have forgotten how to stop their wagons?!

Today's children also have wisdom to offer: One grandchild warned, "Oh, grandma, don't get retired, you'll get retarded." Another presented a daunting challenge: "As soon as grandpa has learned enough, he can retire."

74 / Returning

To return to a location, a city, a book, a person, or whatever, after the passage of much time can be a deeply moving experience, with refreshing or depressing, positive or negative aspects.

Whenever I return to the small town where I grew up, I am constantly amazed at both its strangeness and its familiarity, leaving a dual feeling of being glad I moved on to broader horizons but also being deeply grateful for the nurturing of that community.

When I returned to Oxford, England, after the passage of many years, I eventually found myself amazed at how I walked unerringly to some college or bookstore whose location I seemed to have filed in my memory bank. I recently returned to the campus of the University of Kentucky in Lexington after an absence of literally fifty years, and in a Rip Van Winkle stupor had difficulty focusing in on buildings and scenes, but gradually the vision cleared slightly. What an awesome feeling to know and yet not know these locations, which time has altered and yet preserved.

Veterans returning to Normandy on the fiftieth anniversary of D-Day had many poignant narratives to tell. Each of us have landmark events, wrenching or joyous, to which we return in thought if not in actuality, and their continuity in our consciousness play a significant role in making us who and what we are.

Upon returning to books previously read and underlined, I am impressed anew by the meaningful insight now only vaguely lodging in my memory, but sometimes I wonder what was so special about that underlined passage, for now it seems commonplace—perhaps a sign of one's growth?

Returning to a reconciled state with an alienated friend or family member or colleague can be a glorious and healing moment, a sense of closure and fulfillment, brightening all future moments.

75 / Right-Ness

We live in a world in which "right" is honored and "left" is generally not. We speak of being someone's "right-hand man" or getting on the "right side of" someone. In contrast, we know the negative connotation of a "left-handed compliment."

Tools and facilities—scissors, irons, gear shifts, pencil sharpeners—are made for right-handed people. We take an oath and vote by raising our right hand. People about to be married are asked to join their right hands, we kiss or hug on the right cheek, we shake right hands, and extend our "right hand of fellowship." Children are admonished to eat with their right hand, and in earlier times they were even punished if they ate with their left.

I (Jensen, 1985) have traced numerous examples of right-ness being honorific in Jewish, Christian, and Islamic literature and ritual. In some cultures the right hand is "clean" and the left is "unclean." Thus when under Islamic law a thief is sentenced to have his right hand cut off, it is his only clean hand, hence a double penalty. Biblical literature speaks of sitting on the "right hand of God" and honoring the right hand as being powerful and skillful.

Biblical monarchical metaphors have been continued throughout the centuries as secular monarchies and modern dictatorships all place the second in command or other honored persons on the right side of the king or "Leader."

When one exits a government building in the United States, the Stars and Stripes is supposed to be over one's right shoulder.

While "right-ness" is losing its powerful imagery today, and left-handed people are accommodated more respectfully—especially a valued baseball southpaw!—right-ness still gets preferential treatment. And it's not right!

76 / Roots

Numerous family histories are being constructed, fulfilling the urge to know one's roots. Extensive travels to the home sites in distant countries of one's ancestors are increasingly commonplace. Extensive pamphlets or even books have been created for one's present and future offspring, to let them know from whence they came. Alex Haley's book, *Roots*, and its television production, energized his generation to seek their roots, even if only to some minor degree. Orphans may spend much of their lives trying to discover who their biological parents were.

Something is there that wants to know the soil from whence one grew. It is central to our identity, to our self-knowledge. We are also encouraged to take pride in our origins. But such pride can often contribute to an unhealthy clash with those who spring from different roots and who also take pride in their beginnings. Abe Lincoln is supposed to have said, "I am not so concerned to know how good my grandparents were, as I am in knowing how good their grandson is."

We need to avoid being so preoccupied with knowing and glorying in our roots that we become inward looking, heaping honor and praise on our family tree and almost by definition looking askance at other family trees. We speak of the importance of knowing and taking pride in our long-standing cultural roots, but we ought to be just as eager to know and take pride in the cultural roots of others.

We ought not cling so tightly to the past that we stifle the present and warp the future.

77 / Security

We are living in an increasingly security-conscious society. People lock doors whereas they never used to. Electronic security systems abound in private homes and apartment complexes (and often malfunction!). Women living alone are particularly faced with a heightened fear of intruders. Schools at all levels have security personnel, as do most business institutions and shopping malls. Airports have had to create elaborate, expensive, and time-consuming security measures. Cities and the federal government call for more police on the streets. The simplistic baseball metaphor, "Three strikes and you're out," propels politicians into office and more law breakers into bulging prisons.

Although the cold war has dissipated, the United States and most other nations still spend enormous percentages of their national budgets on armaments, flooding the planet with deadly land mines, chemical and atomic weaponry, in addition to "conventional" armaments. Excessive use of force by police in our cities is documented by video cameras. We are left to feel at times that we need protection from our protectors.

In our scrambling for security from external forces, as important as that is, we ought not overlook the importance of achieving internal security, a sense of living in peace and at ease with ourselves and with others. More ambiguous and more complex in nature, its achievement comes only slowly and imperceptibly. It may be a life-long struggle for some, while others may locate this pearl of great price rather early in life, and others may never find it. Who can measure its cost? Who can measure its value!

78 / Self-Definition

Who are we? What are we? Humans have always sought to define themselves. Family identification is a primary marker, and a common origin of family names in some cultures is to link with the father, that is, we are "John's son"—Johnson. Some cultures do not have family names, but they still identify themselves as the child of so-and-so.

In some cultures, for example in Confucian-dominated areas, the family name is listed first, followed by the individual's name. In Western cultures we highlight the individual by first listing that person's given name, followed by the family name.

People define themselves by larger groupings, such as tribes, clans, villages, areas of land, states or nations, and give primary loyalty to these identifications. Sometimes those loyalties conflict; for example, when people in the former Yugoslavia—that is, southern Slavs—identified themselves by that label, they got along reasonably well, but when they preferred to define themselves by tribal and religious identifications—Croats, Bosnians, Serbs, Muslims, etc.—then they fell to killing and "cleansing" their areas.

People define themselves by their trades and professions, and medieval craft unions were a powerful and satisfying identification for many. People in Western cultures are quick to categorize themselves in this way, and when meeting people for the first time, we probably find ourselves asking, "What do you do?" and then indicate our occupation.

The satisfaction of being able to define ourselves is accompanied by the danger of constructing walls, lines that may be too sharply drawn between ourselves and others. Ultimately, we need to define our individual selves in a way that provides inner equilibrium but does not alienate us from others. Who, or what, are *you*?

79 / Silence

Our talkative culture needs to appreciate more fully the many communicative functions of silence (Jensen, 1973) and to understand that it is not the absence of communication.

It can bind people together or it can separate them. Not only can silence link us with those near to us but also with those removed in distance—a sweetheart, family member, or friend—or time, such as those who have died.

Silence can heal and it can wound. Holding our tongue during agitated moments can be helpful preventive medicine. But we also are aware of the pain inflicted by giving someone the "silent treatment." Silence can shatter a lonely person, but it can soothe a harried young parent. Silence can enable tempers to cool down.

Silence has a way of revealing one's real inner being, by stripping away a veneer, which words may build. Silence may reveal healthy serenity or the sickness of mental derangement.

Silence is employed to register assent, whereby an auditor's silence is taken to mean agreement with the speaker. The sin of silence, seeming to give assent when such was not intended, can leave one with a deep sense of guilt. Silence also registers dissent, and the pages of history reveal many who maintained a courageous and noble silence despite the torture of dungeon, rack or fire.

Throughout history, silence has been associated with a sense of awe, reverence, respect, and mystery; we keep silence at funerals, at beautiful scenes, at some startling event, and during various ceremonies.

The deaf have silence thrust upon them, the monk seeks it out, the overwhelmed executive desperately yearns for it. Many frantically attempt to avoid it. Most of us would profit greatly by engaging in moments of refreshing silence.

80 / Space

Humans desire a reasonable amount of space. We appreciate a house that doesn't cramp our living needs, we may be able to invest in a supplementary lake home, we enjoy space between us and our neighbors. A yard adds facility and beauty to our freedom. We enjoy reasonable counter space in the kitchen, an extra bedroom for guests, and a recreation room in the basement for the family "to spread out." We appreciate a large enough desk on which to work.

Different cultures, to say nothing of different individuals, require more space than others. Cross-cultural communication scholars have analyzed in great detail the science of proxemics, documenting, for example, that some people like to get rather close to the person with whom they are conversing, which may make the second person feel uncomfortably smothered.

City parks provide space for the community, and these "commons" as the British call them, are places where all ages can play and relax at their desired sports and activities. Golf courses provide not only sporting opportunities but a sense of space, of openness, to an otherwise crowded city.

America's Western frontier served as a wide open space for the young nation to spread out, to lessen the crowding on the East Coast (but crowding out the inhabitants who were already in the West!). Cowboy songs glorified the wide open spaces, and a fierce independent spirit resulted.

"Outer space" has in the last half century become a familiar part of our existence and conversation, even if we comprehend little of the scientific aspects.

The essence of freedom and responsibility is expressed in the familiar spatial image that we have freedom to swing our arms but only until they may hit another person. May we have adequate space in our lives, but may we not intrude on the space of others.

81 / Spectator to Participant to Spectator

Impatient youngsters want to move from being spectators to becoming participants. In the small town in which I grew up, I can vividly remember how we looked forward to the day when the high school seniors would be leaving the scene, so we could be the participants on the sporting teams, in the band, etc.

Young people can hardly wait for their sixteenth birthday so they can get in the driver's seat of the family car, can become a *doer* rather than a watcher. Throughout life the same pattern holds, as we yearn to advance from watching others do things, to the stage at which we are permitted to be the actor, can be the licensed electrician, can teach, can manage the company, can be leaders rather than followers in the community.

Wise older folks sense when it is time to retire, to leave the work and the responsibility to younger people. Some older people have a difficult time with this shift, but we need to make that transition gracefully from participant to spectator, for it can be a wonderful fulfillment, an appropriate rounding of the circle of life. We need to glide into the background and watch our children manage affairs, and cheer on the grandchildren in their school studies, sports, music and other activities.

Two of the major social movements of our generation—the civil rights and feminist movements—had at their core this simple and basic desire to become participants rather than spectators in society. Non-whites and women were tired of being sideline spectators, and they wanted and obviously deserved to share in the role of participant.

May we learn to be both good spectators and good participants in life, for indeed there is a time and season for all things.

82 / Sports

Enormous sports stadiums and stratospheric professional sports salaries give testimony to the importance of sports in our culture. Future archaeologists will unearth our contemporary sports facilities and wonder what kind of people we were.

A number of negative things about sports can be cited. School playgrounds and college and university campuses are sometimes accused of taking up an enormously disproportionate amount of space, of dwarfing the educational mission of the institution. Far too much money is spent to benefit mainly a few, and we come to believe sports are more important than they really are. We need to realize that there is something more significant in life than seeing how fast you can run, how high you can jump, or how far you can hit a ball.

But sports at their best minister to many sides of our lives. They build healthy bodies, bolster the mental health of participants and spectators, and provide an exciting unifying social event for schools and communities, and even nations. Healthy values can be strengthened, such as striving after excellence, cooperation with teammates, concentration on a task, rule obedience, fairness, taking care of body and mind. Sports bring together the sexes, all economic levels, all political and religious allegiances, all races, all ages. Crippled grandparents can achieve a close bonding with vigorous grandchildren. Life-long sports such as golf and tennis can be played through many decades.

The great tennis player Arthur Ashe (1993) wrote on his deathbed to his little daughter: "Sports are wonderful; they can bring you comfort and pleasure for the rest of your life. Sports can teach you so much about yourself, your emotions and character, how to be resolute in moments of crisis and how to fight back from the brink of defeat."

83 / Staring

We know it is inappropriate and usually discourteous to stare at people. But there are things at which we ought to stare, if we are to reap the full richness of life around us.

The poet reminds us:

> A poor life this if, full of care,
> We have no time to stand and stare. (Davies, 1939)

We need to take time to stare at the sunrise, the sunset, shadows in early and late hours, the delicate white and ominous dark clouds with their evolving forms. The gentle rain and the violent rainstorm call for our attention. When did you last take time to stare at the shapes and colors and numbers of a flower's petals—I mean really stare? Have you studied the floor covering in a wooded area and various rock formations? We perhaps have stared at the foliage on bushes and trees, but have we been too shy to stare at the naked limbs boldly revealed by a dead tree?

We need to stare at the scurrying ants and squirrels, and at the resting cats and cows. The face of our pet dog has not been thoroughly scrutinized by us during its ten years at our side. Have we stared at the woodpecker ceaselessly and rhythmically drilling like a jack hammer into a chosen morsel? Bird watchers know the pleasure of concentrating through their binoculars on some selected subject.

In a few precious moments, we have followed intensely the actions of a small child. Have we often enough lingered on the perfect moves of an athlete, the grace of a ballet dancer, the disciplined acts of a musician? Art galleries demand more than a swift walk through their collections, and when was the last (or first?) time you carefully stared at that picture hanging on your living room wall for lo these many years?

To enrich our lives, we indeed need to take time to stare.

90

84 / Strangers

One of the important merits of traveling in a foreign land is to experience what it is like to be a stranger. To be an "outsider" with all its insecurity, anxiety, and vulnerability is a significant psychological happening of great worth, even if it brings considerable pain.

Many also know the pain of being "outsiders" in their own families, in their workplaces, or in their various organizations where they hold views and values divergent from the group. They are strangers in their own land.

Ancient literature, usually tribal in origin, pays tribute to the parochial "in-group" and warns against outsiders. That's what lends power to the story of the Good Samaritan, for the hero is a foreigner, a member of a despised out-group. Confucian emphasis is on treating with compassion the "in-group," but similar obligations do not extend toward strangers. It came to be challenged by Mohism, which emphasized that one should show love to all, including strangers.

It is understandable why strangers have through the centuries been held at an arm's length. They are an unknown factor, they have different characteristics, ways, and values. They often enter our territory without permission, wander through our land with suspicion, and exit sometimes with our valuables. There has not been established a bond of trust.

We are experiencing a growing number of "strangers" in our midst—immigrants, foreign students, employees transferred to new locations. We need to interact with them with love, as we would hope they would do if we were the sojourners, for it will bring a mutual enrichment to all our lives. As Elie Wiesel (1990) has written: "Man, by definition, is born a stranger: coming from nowhere, he is thrust into an alien world which existed before him. . . . And which will survive him."

85 / Tastes

It is interesting to note how our tastes for different foods and drinks change through the years. Those high on our preference list one year may be low in later years, and vice versa. Going on a rigid diet often brings a surprising change in tastes. I certainly found that to be true with my cholesterol-reducing diet, gradually discovering that fatty foods no longer had their former appeal.

The same dynamic is present in our intellectual and moral tastes. Our strong high school interests gradually change into areas more important and rewarding as we mature, especially if we continue on to college and graduate school. We do not regret leaving our "low-vaulted past," for we move into far richer domains. We are not "sacrificing," for we see vistas more satisfying and more significant.

People need to make sure they are not just marking time, stuck at immature plateaus. They need to develop their intellectual and moral tastes, and they need to see the harm in being hooked on the "great taste" of such things as tobacco, drugs, alcohol, and other debilitating habits causing harm to themselves and others. Even "couch potatoes" may discover that participating in sports or other activities is a pleasant plus, far more satisfying than passively sponging up the tube offerings.

Charles Darwin late in life wrote in his autobiography (Barlow, 1958): "Looking backwards, I can now perceive how my love for science gradually preponderated over every other taste. During the first two years [at Cambridge University] my old passion for shooting survived in nearly full force, and I shot myself all the birds and animals for my collection; but gradually I gave up my gun more and more, and finally altogether . . . as shooting interfered with my work. . . . I discovered, though unconsciously and insensibly, that the pleasure of observing and reasoning was a much higher one than that of skill and sport. The primeval instincts of barbarian slowly yielded to the acquired tastes of the civilized man" (pp. 78-79).

86 / Teachers

At their best, teachers do many valuable things. They are speakers and they are writers. They dispense information, they discover new information, they discover new relationships between old ideas, they correct the work of others, they advise, they develop and refine skills, they inspire, they reduce ignorance, they magnify the will to learn, they facilitate interaction, they strengthen the weak and weaken the arrogant. They question questionable claims and formulate better ones. They awaken dormant qualities in their students, squeezing out the best that is in them, helping them to become what they are now but have potential for becoming. I won't list what teachers are at their worst!

Research professors willingly submit their findings to the public scrutiny of their peers in publications and conferences, and realize the truth of the remark of the ancient writer of Ecclesiastes (7:5): "It is better to hear the rebuke of the wise, than for a man to hear the song of fools."

In this trying but immensely satisfying occupation, teachers will probably make an adequate income but will not become wildly wealthy. Instead of making millions, they will mold thousands. The committed teacher will be able to echo the testimony of Confucius (VII, 2, Waley, p. 123): "I have never grown tired of learning nor wearied of teaching others what I have learnt." Committed teachers at all levels seek to improve their teaching and seek to deepen their bonding with teachers all over the world in their common enterprise.

In contemporary higher education, it is now wisely common for students to have the opportunity to evaluate their professors. One hopes that the following anecdote is apocryphal: It is said that in the famous medieval Bologna University in Italy, one professor was such a poor lecturer that finally the students rushed him with quills poised and stabbed him to death! At least their evaluation was unambiguous!

94

87 / Time

We "waste," "save," "steal," "mark," and "use" time. We seek to "fill" time with meaningful activities, and "give" time to worthy projects. Time is a commodity, especially in Western cultures. We insist on beginning and terminating meetings on time, on being on time for appointments, on respecting the time of others. We resent it when people infringe on our time.

But the feeling that time is precious and is to be highly valued is universal. For example, there is an apt and beautiful ancient Chinese saying that "an inch of time is an inch of gold."

Humans construct arbitrary time grids—hours, days, years, centuries. Fiscal years and academic years have as much meaning as chronological years.

Time often serves as a handy scapegoat. Administrators sometimes say they would have been glad to consult with their staff, but there "just wasn't time." A convenient "out" from considering some new policy is to suggest that while it may be a good idea, there just isn't enough time to examine and implement it. We ease our consciences by claiming we would have liked to help others in need, but we just didn't have enough time. We claim we cannot undertake a certain task because we just can't meet a given "deadline"—an ominous metaphor.

Many people find it extremely difficult to balance their time satisfactorily between work and family, with the latter usually getting left out. Yet, have you ever heard of persons on their deathbed uttering, "Oh, I wish I had spent more time at the office!" Too late we see our unbalanced handling of the time given us on this earth. Small children plead, often nonverbally, with their busy parents, "Give me more of your time." How sad when parents don't give that most precious of gifts.

Surely it can be said that how we use time goes far to define who and what we are.

88 / Reaching the Top

What do you say and do when you have reached your designated goal, when you have reached the top of the mountain? The Zen Buddhist probably says: "Keep climbing." The CEO says, "Keep control of things." The altruist says, "Now I can give to others." The pessimist says, "It wasn't worth the climb." The poet says, "Let's rest and absorb the beauty." The activist says, "Let's climb that other mountain over there."

We all have climbed, or will climb, mountains of some importance, and hopefully we want to be able to look back and say: "It was a good choice, I'm glad I did it, I have a feeling of accomplishment, I have been strengthened, I have helped others along the way, I have absorbed the beauty, I have realized that there may be other mountains to climb."

After the historic multiracial election in 1994 in South Africa, President F. W. de Klerk's concession speech included the following: "Mr. Mandela has walked a long road and now stands at the top of the hill. A traveler would sit down and admire the view. But a man of destiny knows that beyond this hill lies another and another. The journey is never complete" (*Manchester Guardian*, 1994, p. 4).

How to descend from the top? Many people find it easy and comfortable to turn over responsibilities to others and to enjoy the relaxing unwinding process. Others find it traumatic to leave the peak, to realize that they are not indispensable, that their role can be filled by those who follow. Surely we need to learn to descend as gracefully as possible.

Great civilizations—Egyptian, Greek, Roman, Inca, Aztec—have melted down to shadows. Perhaps humans, as civilizations or as individuals, aren't meant to stay at the top?

89 / Transplanting

As a youngster I had the responsibility of caring for our potato field, and in one corner, a small wild rose bush kept appearing. For a couple of years it was simply a weed to me, and I hoed it down, but I didn't kill it.

One year I finally dug it up and transplanted it to our front yard. No longer defined as a troublesome weed in its new location, it became instead a lovely perennial flowering bush.

Some "weeds" in life can become lovely flowers. Some youngsters defined as "misfits" in family, school, and society may flower and mature in different surroundings, in different soil. May we constantly be on the alert to see this potential all around us, as we help young people grow and find their niche in life.

Various transplanted items may bring special pleasure in their new settings. Our son transplanted some small aspen trees from our lake cottage to his city home, and our daughter transplanted some lilac bushes from our city family home where she grew up, to her home where her family is now growing up. When we did some reconstruction to our city home, we freed up a door and window, which could be used in reconstructing our lake cottage. These transplants have brought not only beauty but are also tangible linkages with other places and long-time loving memories.

People as well as flowers, trees, bushes, and objects are often transplanted. Refugees and immigrants are transplants, some temporary and some permanent. Transplants need some initial special tender-loving-care while they are adjusting to their new soil and habitat. Some transplants flourish and some do not. We should do our part in helping to nourish these transplants to sink their roots firmly in their new soil.

Humans are social beings. To be fully human, we need and desire interaction with other humans. What makes those interactions fulfilling is trust. Families, organizations, communities, and nations all need trust as the cement for their cohesiveness.

Insightful observations on the importance of trust have spanned the centuries. Confucius, for example, asserted: "I do not see what use a man can be put to, whose word cannot be trusted" (Waley, 1938, 11:22). Dietrich Bonhoeffer (1972) wrote during his imprisonment by the Nazis. "Trust will always be one of the greatest, rarest, and happiest blessings of our life in community. ... Without trust, life is impoverished" (pp. 12, 29). Vaclav Havel (1992) has written: "There is nothing worse than having people you care about begin to lose faith in you" (p. 229).

Wise trust must be built gradually and thoughtfully. It must be earned; it must be reciprocal. Trust is to be demonstrated by actions, not mere words. It enables us to predict future actions. Trust is strong yet delicate, like a thread that holds two entities together. Once broken, trust is extremely difficult to rebuild.

Trust is a gamble, a risk that those who have suffered from misplaced trust know to their sorrow. The danger of granting blind trust is indeed great, and in group-think contexts, the members of a small group unwittingly abdicate their critical powers, placing complete trust in "the group," which they feel can do no wrong. Blind trust in charismatic leaders, be they in the field of religion, politics, business, or in other walks of life, can lead to disastrous results.

Some wit has said, the trouble with the world is that half of the people don't know, and the other half do but can't be trusted.

91 / Truthfulness

What a central factor is truth in the ongoing relationships among humans! Except for those few who actually enjoy misleading people, most of us place truthfulness at the top of our ethical concerns and commitments. The ancient Persians felt that "the most disgraceful thing in the world . . . is to tell a lie" (Herodotus, 1947, p. 77), and that has generally echoed down through the centuries.

We are uplifted and strengthened by such assurances that "the truth shall make you free" (John 8:32). Free indeed—from the cruelties of ignorance and superstition and fear. Academic institutions enshrine on their buildings and in their literature that they are a part of that grand enterprise to search for truth.

When people assert that they "have arrived" at the truth, have concluded their search, that is when one can well be wary of them. Their game plan from then on is to induce others to accept "the truth," get others to conform, to accept without question, or suffer charges of heresy, disloyalty, or stupidity. Those who assert that they know "the truth" need to harbor at least in one small corner of their mind the idea that they may indeed be wrong.

It is important to realize that truth is composed of the two components of accuracy and completeness. We may indeed be accurate—truthful—but incomplete—untruthful—in our message, and vice versa. Parents, employers, teachers, government officials, military personnel, and others usually have to carry out their duties on less than complete information, even though what they do have is accurate.

A wise magazine editor (*Colliers*, 1912, April 27) once wrote that truth "comes like light and sweet breezes, to those whose hands are busy, whose minds are open, whose hearts are kind" (p. 8).

92 / Upness

Humans have historically acquired great inspiration from heights, from mountains, from upness. We revel in the long vistas in the high elevations. Religious literature speaks of going down into a hell and up into a heaven. We are encouraged to keep our chin *up*, we work hard to get *up* in the world. We feel *down in the dumps*, we lament being *under the weather*. Up is good, down is bad.

Church steeples pierce the heights in a symbolic thrust toward God. A person recently stole a car in a parking ramp, which had the keys in it, drove to the top of the ramp, where the police apprehended him. He said he only wanted to get closer to God—it was, after all, Holy Week! In Bali the good spirits are up in the mountains, the bad spirits are down in the ocean. The ancient Persians and many Mediterranean peoples historically went up into the highest mountains to offer sacrifices to their gods.

Needle-shaped secular buildings "scrape the sky" in their pronouncement of greatness. The American skyscrapers became a symbol of the young nation's urge to excel over the old world of Europe, and now the twin-tower skyscraper in Kuala Lumpur, Malaysia, becomes the highest structure in the world, but soon to be overtaken by Shanghai, Hong Kong, and other cities. This Asian surge to excel over the United States and Europe, to build higher and higher structures (which may not be architecturally or functionally successful), continues the habit of succumbing to upness, repeating personal, professional, and national vanity.

Will there come a time when we reverse the metaphor and think of "downness" as good, for we do look to underground transportation networks and shopping malls and tunnels not only for efficiency and convenience but also for safety in case of bombing or storms. To save energy costs, we increasingly "build" structures underground. Will our descendants look to excavated areas "from whence cometh their help?"

93 / Values

Throughout the centuries conscientious human beings have been searching for and seeking to live up to the highest values in life. What is the *summum bonum*, the highest good? Today we keep asking that eternal question. Truth, justice, love, freedom, tolerance, peace, and righteousness make the list of most people. The resounding assertion of the ancient Hebrew prophet has guided many: "to do justly, . . . to love kindness, and to walk humbly with thy God" (Micah, 6:8).

We challenge ourselves to focus on the inner spirit rather than on such externalities as dietary conformities, observance of rules, specific clothing and hair grooming, sacrificial acts, money giving, or constructing religious edifices. It is the inner attitude that counts.

In recent years there has been a concerted effort to teach values in our schools at every level. This commendable emphasis does have potential drawbacks, but nevertheless is a healthy reminder that to attain full maturity, we need to develop our moral side as well as the intellectual.

Seldom do values operate in isolation; it is the mix of values with which we grapple in our moral dilemmas, as we try to determine which value takes precedence in a given situation. Often it is the clash of two "good" values; for example, freedom of expression may bump up against responsibility for communal peace and order. Furthermore, the courage of a bank thief or the sincerity of a demagogue illustrate that good values can be employed in the service of bad ends. "Obedience," a "good" value, may be very dangerous if harnessed by some authoritarian regime.

Some societies and cultures are identified by core values. It is often said that Americans are defined and bound together by a set of values, not by ethnicity, religion, or class. We honor, freedom, individualism, private initiative, volunteerism, and self-governance. Values are not, however, always easy to put in practice.

94 / Walls

Humans have built walls throughout history. Ancient and medieval cities enclosed themselves with thick stone walls for protection from "outsiders." The Great Wall of China and the Maginot Line in France sought to protect a nation from invasion by outside enemies. Some walls, for example the Berlin Wall or prison walls, seek to stop inhabitants from getting out. There comes a time when walls come tumbling down, be they contemporary Berlin or ancient Jericho.

Some walls have been constructed as memorials, such as the Vietnam Memorial in Washington, D.C., the World War II memorial in Okinawa, the Civil Rights Memorial in Montgomery, Alabama, and the American Immigrant Wall of Honor at the Ellis Island Immigration Museum.

Some walls have religious functions, such as the Wailing Wall in Jerusalem, or the intangible "walls" of excluding non-believers from places of worship, or of forbidding intermarriage with other religions.

Nations build "walls" at their borders and do not permit noncitizens to enter without certain documents. Through the "wall" of censoring mass media, some nations seek to protect their citizens from "decadent" and "dangerous" moral and political ideas. Many tightly knit groups build walls of separation from outsiders. We as individuals build psychological walls to protect our privacy or to isolate ourselves from foreign ideas.

Neighbors build walls and fences, with both positive and negative symbolism. As the poet Robert Frost (1969) in his familiar "Mending Wall" has his neighbor express it: "Good fences make good neighbors." But Frost feels:

103

Before I build a wall I'd ask to know
What I was walling in or walling out,
And to whom I was like to give offense.
Something there is that doesn't love a wall,
That wants it down.

95 / Water

Humans, animals, and plants all search continually for that essential ingredient for life—water. Scientists point out that water needs to be determined to be present on Mars if there is to be life there. Here in most parts of the United States, we take our water for granted, with safe hot and cold water coming effortlessly from faucets and with being given a free glass of cool water with our restaurant meals. But I have certainly not forgotten the days of my youth when I had to pump our water from our own well and heat water on the cook stove.

In some parts of the country at certain times, too little water can cause great worry, as reservoirs sink dangerously low, and farmers' parched lands lower acreage output and raise consumer prices.

But too much water likewise is to be feared. Witness those who try to cope with flooded houses, fields, and roads. Dead trees standing lonely with wet feet and naked torsos on lake shores speak to the effects of too much water.

It is necessary to balance the blessing of sufficient water with the appreciation of not having too much. Adjusting to the annual rhythm of rainfall in some parts of the world is a central task for many people. For example, the monsoon season in south and southeast Asia from June to October at first brings a glorious relief from the hot, parched, dry months of March through May, but it is not long before muddy roads, moldy and soggy conditions, and the depressing absence of the sun cause one to yearn for the end of the rainy season.

Water is employed as an important life-giving symbol. Religious baptism depends on water, and literature abounds in water metaphors depicting cleansing.

Indeed, the coming together of two parts of hydrogen with one part of oxygen is an awesome phenomenon. Inhabitants of this planet in the twenty-first century will need to manage wisely this central ingredient to the existence of what we call life.

96 / The Way

"Taoism" means "the way." Christianity and other religions likewise pronounce a core emphasis as their "way," which their adherents are admonished to follow and which serves to define them.

Secular "ways" are all around us too. Small towns and large corporations may have an unwritten understanding that "that is the way we do things here." Children are often confronted with: "that is just the way our family does it." Teenage gangs impose a rigid code on their members. Nations pride themselves in their "way," their culture, for example, "the American way." Academic institutions devote themselves to developing a "way," a special emphasis, which marks their graduates, such as openmindedness, an international outlook, a rigorous reasoning capacity, a life of service to others.

These "ways" have the potential for building the finest of human beings. The result can be mature, insightful, compassionate, cooperative, and loyal persons.

But the potential for unfortunate products is also present. Religious "ways" can become dogmatic, unthinking, even cruel, mindsets. Small-town mores may breed "small town" provincialism. Corporate cultures may force loyalty to questionable company practices, to the detriment of individual employees and the general public. Rigid family traditions may produce warped offspring, insecure in outside contexts. Nations may create cowed and unthinking citizens, as can various gang structures.

The notion of a "way" is of course rooted in the journey metaphor, indicating that as one goes through life and goes about one's day-to-day activities, one should manifest a certain "way" of life, should reveal a consistent manner of behaving. Woe unto us if these "ways" have serious flaws. But we can rejoice if our "way" brings fulfillment and well-being to ourselves and to the larger society.

97 / Weaving

One of the most common and most meaningful metaphors in life is the image of weaving. Surely watching an expert working at a weaver's loom entrenches the power of the weaving metaphor, causing us to marvel at the ability to create a beautiful fabric from isolated threads. Clothing stores are filled with many such beautifully woven garments.

Members of family realize that their lives are intimately woven together, that each represents a strand in that particular unit. Members of small groups and large organizations that have a strong cohesiveness likewise sense that their efforts and contributions are woven together with other members, thus achieving some specific product or general outcome. Countries say that their nationhood is a delicate and rich fabric woven through many years, sometimes centuries. Honoring individuality as we do in the United States, we at the same time realize that we must be willing and able to intertwine our individual efforts with those of others in order to achieve meaningful outcomes in our complex modern society.

Intercultural studies emphasize that we should respect the fabrics woven by other cultures, even though we may think they are strange. The 1995 UN Conference on Women in Beijing illustrated both the beauty of many varied societal fabrics coming together but also the tensions between those societies that view the public role and behavior of women in vastly different ways.

Indeed, why should we respect political or religious totalitarian fabrics? Why should we respect an entrenched apartheid society? Just because such fabrics have managed to be created does not mean they should continue to exist. Some fabrics deserve to be torn and discarded; others deserve to be honored and maintained. Which, of course, brings us to the task of judgment. We must choose our woven societal garments, and much hangs in the balance of our choosing.

98 / Withdrawal

To withdraw, to detach oneself from current contexts, has been a central contribution to personal and societal health and enrichment throughout the centuries. Ancients and contemporaries seeking to become better attuned to eternal values and perspective have intentionally withdrawn to the wilderness, literally or figuratively. Various religious orientations have sought deeper inner peace, insight, and commitment via a lengthy withdrawal from the general society.

The notion of a fixed time, such as forty days and forty nights in the wilderness, or a retreat for a weekend or a week, or a lifetime in a monastery, has been imbedded in the human experience. The farm lad who, deeply desiring more education, decides to leave the plowing of the fields and retreats into the four-year secular monastery of a university, has much similarity to the religiously inspired youth who enters a monastic order. Indeed, both the scholarly and religious life demand some period of withdrawal.

Withdrawal to some treatment center is basic for those who seek to become freed from the clutches of drug or alcohol abuse. All of us can enter into a healthy withdrawal by a quiet weekend at the lake, by brief moments of quietness amongst the crowds around us, by immersing ourselves in some reading.

But it is important to come away from moments or years of withdrawal to return something of value to the larger human community. In drinking at the well of solitude, we ought not to become drunk with our withdrawal, falling into a passive stupor, becoming spiritual or intellectual couch-potatoes.

The pouting child or the frazzled parent often need to retreat to some room for aloneness and healing, but they should reemerge eventually with great inner fiber and richness of character.

From detachment to richer attachment should be the goal of withdrawing.

99 / Work

Some hate it. Some love it. Some just put up with it. For humans to survive, work has to be done by someone. Young children and the destitute live by the work of others, but most adults on this planet are expected to live by their own labor.

It has been said that if you choose a job that you like, you will never have to work! Indeed, getting paid for what one likes to do is truly a wonderful blessing. When one enjoys going to work each day, one is indeed a rich person, regardless of the size of the paycheck! Work can give dignity and meaning to a person's life, creating a sense of self-worth and self-esteem.

Rooted in many cultures and religions is a strong work ethic, which takes pride in work, which says that to use one's life in some productive fashion is indeed praiseworthy and is fulfilling one's obligation to society. Confucianism for centuries has fueled the Chinese talent and dependability in workmanship. American history is intimately linked with the energy and sense of responsibility of the Protestant work ethic, emphasizing that we were put on earth by the Creator for the purpose of doing something worthwhile with our lives, and the dogged determination of the immigrant to seize the opportunities in their new world.

There is of course the sad spectacle of the "workaholic," one who with blinders shuts out family and all other obligations and pleasures for the singular focus on one's job.

I would suggest the following *modus operandi*: (1) Work as if the very existence of the world depended on your doing your task as thoroughly and as well as possible. (2) Complete the job—tie the knot—don't leave it "almost done." (3) Sit back and laugh at yourself; realize that the world will probably continue rather well, thank you, without your input. (4) Don't do #3 before #1 and #2.

100 / Writing

In my retirement I am often asked, "What are you doing?" When I say I am writing a couple of books, the follow-up question not infrequently is, "But what are you *really* doing?" Writing does not equal "doing." Small children continually disrupt their parents who are writing at the desk or table, for parents are perceived as not "doing" anything, in contrast to vacuuming, cooking, gardening, etc.

Despite the agony of creating, the plain hard work of gathering, conceptualizing, organizing, writing and re-writing, the act of writing does bring great pleasure. There is usually a wonderful feeling of accomplishment, as there is in any other creative endeavor. Where "nothing" was, where there was only a void, there now is "something"—a book, an article, an essay, a poem, a letter.

Why does one write? Authors of course will give varying answers. Some would say it is simply to "get out" those thoughts that are in their consciousness. People write to persuade, to inform, to amuse, to edify their readers. Some write to comfort their readers, some to afflict the comforted. Great writers burrow into our inner beings whether we like it or not. Some write to an immediate audience, some aim to make an impact on readers in some distant time and place.

One important and perhaps overlooked benefit to writing is that one comes to read other books and articles, etc., with greater insight and awareness of what has gone into the organization, the idea development, the choices of vocabulary and style. In short, one's reading is enriched.

A few observers—only a few, I hope—may share the gloomy spirit of Ecclesiastes (12:12): "of making many books there is no end." I hope this small volume was a worthwhile read, a useful and uplifting skip through some of life's experiences.

References

American Revision Committee. (1901). *The Holy Bible*. New York: Thomas Nelson & Sons.

Ashe, A. & Rampersad, A. (1993). *Days of Grace: A Memoir*. New York: Knopf.

Augustine, Saint (of Hippo). (1949). *The Confessions of Saint Augustine*. (E.B. Pusey, Trans.). New York: Modern Library.

Barlow, N. (Ed.) (1958). *The Autobiography of Charles Darwin*. London: Collins.

Bonhoeffer, D. (1972). *Letters and Papers from Prison*. (E. Bethge, Trans. and Ed.). New York: Macmillan. (Original work published 1951).

Confucius. (1938). *The Analects of Confucius*. (A. Waley Trans.). New York: Vintage Books.

Davies, W. H. (1939). Leisure. In G. K. Anderson & E. L. Walton (Eds.), *This Generation* (pp. 133–134). Chicago: Scott, Foresman.

Frost, R. (1939). Mending wall. In G. K. Anderson & E. L. Walton (Eds.), *This Generation* (pp. 61–62). Chicago: Scott, Foresman.

Fukuzawa, Y. (1960). *The Autobiography of Fukuzawa Yukichi*. (E. Kiyooka, Trans.). Tokyo: The Hokuseido Press. (First edition, 1934).

Gandhi, S. (Ed.) (1992). *Two Alone, Two Together*. London: Hodder Stoughton.

Gibran, K. (1973). *The Prophet*. New York: Alfred Knopf.

Harris, M. H. (Trans.) (1901). *Hebraic Literature: Translations from the Talmud, Midrashim and Kabbala*. New York: M. Walter Dunne.

Havel, V. (1992). *Open letters: Selected Writings. 1965–1990* (P. Wilson, Ed.), New York: Vintage Books.

Jensen, J. V. (1973). Communicative Functions of Silence. *Etc. A Review of General Semantics*, 30: 249–257.

Jensen, J. V. (1985). Religious roots for right-handedness. *World Communication*. 14: 129–135.

Kantar, M. J. (1990). *Children's responses to televised adaptations of literature*. Unpublished doctoral dissertation, University of Minnesota, Minneapolis.

King, M. L., Jr. (1967). *The Trumpet of Conscience*. New York: Harper & Row.

Lloyd, George D. (1960). A scrap of paper, September 21, 1914. In E. Rhys (Ed.), *British Orations: From Ethelbert to Churchill* (pp. 341–350). London: J. M. Dent Sons.

Manchester Guardian Weekly (England). (1994, May 8) p. 4.

Merton, T. (1959). *The Silent Life*. New York: Farrar, Straus & Cudahy.

Ramacharaka, Y. (Ed.) (1935). *The Bhagavad Gita*.. Chicago: The Yogi Publication Society.

Tagore. (1961). *A Tagore Reader*. (A. Chakravarty, Ed.) Boston: Beacon Press.

Thucydides. (1934). *The Complete Writings of Thucydides: The Peloponnesian War*. (R. Crawley, Ed.) New York: Modern Library. (Originally published, 1876.)

Tuan, Y. (1977). *Space and Place: The Perspective of Experience*. Minneapolis: University of Minnesota Press.

Whatley, R. (1963). *Elements of Rhetoric*. (D. Ehninger, Ed.) Carbondale, Illinois: Southern Illinois University Press. (Originally published, 1828).

Whittier, J. G. (1892). *Poetical Works*. Boston: Houghton Mifflin.

Wiesel, E. (1990). *From the Kingdom of Memory: Reminiscences*. New York: Summit Books.